INCARNATION

INCARNATION
Jon L. Berquist

SABBATH AND JUBILEE
Richard H. Lowery

INCARNATION

JON L. BERQUIST

St. Louis, Missouri

All scripture quotations, unless otherwise indicated, are from the *New Revised Standard Version Bible*, copyright 1989, Division of Christian Education of the National Council of the Churches of Christ in the United States of America. Used by permission. All rights reserved.

Cover and interior design: Elizabeth Wright
Art direction: Elizabeth Wright

This book is printed on acid-free, recycled paper.

Visit Chalice Press on the World Wide Web at
www.chalicepress.com

10 9 8 7 6 5 4 3 2 1   00 01 02 03 04

Library of Congress Cataloging–in–Publication Data

Berquist, Jon L.
    Incarnation / Jon L. Berquist
        p.   cm. — (Understanding biblical themes)
    Includes index.
    ISBN 0-8272-3825-8
    1. Incarnation–Biblical teaching. 2. Presence of God–Biblical teaching. I. Title.
II. Series.
BT220.B46 1999
232'.1 — dc21   99-050543
                                                      CIP
Printed in the United States of America

In memory of Harriet

CONTENTS

PREFACE

One of my earliest religious memories is reading Luke 2, the story of Jesus' birth in a Bethlehem stable. In that story I found my introduction to incarnation. God was present in a special way in Jesus, at a particular point in history and in a specific context. Here I first learned to marvel at the way God is embodied and related to the groundedness of the real world, even if an ancient world set in Luke's narrative telling of Jesus' life. I also gained an appreciation for the many ways that people responded to Jesus in that story. From that beginning, I became interested in the variety of ways that God was present in biblical texts, and the many different understandings that people have had of God and Jesus in the rest of the Bible. Eventually, my fascination extended to those who were not able to sense God's presence and to the realization that we, like biblical characters, struggle to make sense of our experience of God in the world.

This book has afforded me an opportunity to bring together many of these themes and interests. As such, it is a highly personal book, sharing in my own attempts to relate to God and to speak of that relationship to others. The book also attempts to deal with the range of the Bible's interest in God's presence (and absence) and to explore through these biblical texts the nature of relationship with God. Like all relationships, our life with God is a thing of beauty and mystery, full of joy, uncertainty, frustration, assurance, hope, desire, and dreams for the future. One never knows quite what to say, for words do not encapsulate any relationship. No matter what one says, there are other things remaining to say. Thus, the various chapters present different aspects of this relationship in ways that might seem contradictory, but that is because our relationship with God is so hard to describe. There is always more to be said—and in the end, relationships can be more real than any explanation.

I am particularly indebted to Ronald J. Allen, Jacquelyn L. Foster, David P. Polk, Patrice L. Rosner, Larry A. Thomas, and David C. Waggoner for their comments and discussion at various stages of this book's development. I am also grateful to many friends whose care and support uphold me daily and whose encouragement for this project at particular times has enabled me to continue. Although any list would be partial, I wish to mention A. K. M. and Margaret Adam, Lori G. Beaman, Mary Beth and Richard J. Berquist, L. Susan Bond, Rebecca Button Prichard, Nancy J. Ramsay, and Joseph M. Webb. My thanks also go to those groups who have graciously provided opportunities to try some of this material in public before it was ready for print: ministers' retreats within the Christian Church (Disciples of Christ) and United Church of Christ in Colorado in October 1995, and in the Nebraska panhandle in February 1997; and an adult Sunday school class at Compton Heights Christian Church (Disciples of Christ) in St. Louis during the fall of 1998.

Writings always reflect their contexts. While I have been working on this project, I have been nurtured by my wonderful colleagues at Christian Board of Publication and Chalice Press, as well as by the faith community at Compton Heights Christian Church. I have been spurred in my thinking about incarnation—and in much of the rest of life—by my regular conversations with Ron Allen, who knows how to goad and sustain at the same time. During my hours at the computer, my closest companions have been Harriet, Tweedy, and Joseph, who have taught me much about embodied life and have frequently reminded me of the many good reasons to leave the keyboard for a while.

Harriet died in August of 1999, just a few weeks after I completed this book. We had shared eight wonderful, even if tumultuous, years together, and we experienced joy in them all. She lasted through her twelfth year, a full life for an Airedale, and she modeled a tender persistence to the end.

INTRODUCTION

C hristian faith has always been a biblical faith. The role of scripture in shaping faith is one of the most enduring characteristics of Christianity. Calling Christians a people of the Book or followers of the Word is perfectly appropriate; the Bible is the source of our belief. Scripture is where we meet God. From the theological statements of church leaders to the daily and weekly practices of believers worldwide, the Bible remains central to our Christian identity and to our relationship with God.

But the book isn't everything.

At the core of our faith, we relate to God in a way that is far from bookish. We know God personally, intimately, not just through the written words of our tradition. We do not just read about God; the value of scripture in Christian life is that it can start a relationship with God.

Our faith involves our bodies, not merely our minds. People have seen God and touched God. In Jesus—and in many other ways— God has been among us in the flesh. Our relationship with God is not just words; it is the real life of embodied beings. We are made in God's image, and God enters into human flesh. We enter into this relationship with minds, hearts, souls, and bodies. This is the way God loves us, and the way we love God.

1

The embodiedness of our relationship with God is like the other relationships of our lives. Relationships grow with time together, time to see each other and even perhaps to touch each other. Even in this high-tech world of a new millennium, we still long for ways to see and touch each other, to sense with our eyes and ears and hands the embodiedness of our lives. Letters, phone calls, and e-mails are important ways to keep relationships alive. Many relationships could not survive without them, and some relationships never would have started without these technologies. But there remains a need for bodies, to see and touch each other. So air traffic increases each year, and the roads fill up at Christmas and other holidays as people travel to be together, to have the relational connections possible only when bodies are in the same room. The intensity of relationship we seek, whether with friends, with family, with partners, or with lovers, requires being together.

So what about God? How do we have an embodied relationship with God? How is God physically present in our lives? We do not see God in our own lives, not as a physical body, a human person who walks among us each day. Even though our tradition promises that God is truly with us, it also echoes the sounds of God's absence. One of our hymns teaches us to sing to the "immortal, invisible, God only wise, in light inaccessible hid from our eyes." Such a God is not in bodies like ours; such a God cannot be seen, let alone touched. "No one has ever seen God," says John 1:18, which then goes on to mention one way that God is made known to us.[1] But even though our heritage makes such sweeping claims, the Bible contains numerous stories of how God is physically present with and intimately visible to humans.

Moses was one of those people, according to the Bible, who saw God. Exodus 33:11 contains the remarkable sentence: "The LORD used to speak to Moses face to face, as one speaks to a friend." If God is willing to be seen by some, then why not by us all? We want to see God. Even when it seems difficult or even impossible, we search for ways to see God. We are like lovers, longing for the glimpse of the beloved. We wait for God as we wait at a bus stop or an airport, or as we wait at our front doors when we know someone we love is about

---

[1] Biblical quotations are from the *New Revised Standard Version*, unless otherwise marked. In some cases, the wording has been altered for inclusive language.

to come by. We wait; we pace; we listen for any sound that our loved one is approaching. We want to see, and when we see, we want to touch, to hold our loved one close and feel the warmth. We desire to see God. Throughout scripture, there are glimpses of God, and we long for a chance to see God again, face to face, as Moses did.

Some will wonder if we should take the stories of God's body literally or not. Maybe they are just striking figures of speech. Perhaps these stories are merely human attempts to personify God. But these stories paint a vivid picture that compels us to see with these writers' eyes and to consider how their depiction of God shows us our own faith. For some, this will require a suspension of disbelief, or at least a conscious exercise of the imagination. For many, it will mean thinking beyond the strictures of some previously held beliefs to listen to the simple and surprising claims of biblical texts. The ancient writers of the Bible believed in God's body more than we do, and when we read their writings, their belief may prove to be contagious. We may not believe the same things they do, but we may well believe more deeply.

Does God really have a body or is it all just a story—that is not the right question. Figures of speech are not to be disregarded; they can alter perceptions and change our lives. Instead, we should ask, "What difference does it make?" Will these stories, literal or not, give us a new vitality in relationship with God, whose presence we may well sense more clearly?

This book is about seeing God. In scripture, God lived in physical form, and perhaps we can see God today. The book is also about vision and touching, for we know that when we see God, we will want to rush into God's arms. Seeing God and touching God will touch us deep within; our lives will never be the same.

We will explore the biblical stories, poems, and texts in which God was visible. This book concentrates on the Bible and takes seriously its ideas about God. In this task of biblical theology, we will keep one eye on scripture, while the other eye searches our own lives for signs of God's presence. This requires the honesty to admit that often we only sense God as absent from our lives. The theological traditions that have come after the Bible both affirm and deny that God has a body. Biblical texts offer a variety of views on this topic, providing ground for many different theological claims.

Chapter 1 begins our investigation with the biblical texts that claim God's literal, physical presence. When God walks among humans in the garden of Eden, there's no indication that the text is being metaphorical or is speaking of a spiritual presence. To the contrary— God is physically present. God sees the people with physical eyes, walks among them with physical legs, and makes clothing for them with physical hands. God has a body in the story of the garden of Eden. Beyond that story, the Bible has many other accounts of when God lived among the people on earth with a physical body. This is where we start our biblical understanding of God's incarnation.

In chapter 2, we focus on passages about how God is present through other people, especially through the leaders of Israel. In the New Testament, this idea continues. God keeps sending people as ambassadors—to make God's presence real and physically embodied through the bodies of human followers.

God is also present through the spirit, and chapter 3 explores this idea of how God is present with people. Prayer is a form of spiritual presence also, because it is a way of feeling that God is near—even if God is nowhere to be seen at the moment. In our own world, we are used to various ways in which we can feel close to people even across distances, such as telephones, letters, memories, and e-mail. In similar fashion, we can feel and sense the presence of God's body even when we cannot see God physically.

Any time we have a relationship with someone, we prefer to concentrate on the good parts. But things are never that easy in real life. Even in our relationships with God, there are times that God's presence (whether physical or spiritual) feels dangerous to us. In chapter 4, we will look at biblical texts where God's presence was threatening, and where people did not necessarily want God to be physically present.

God's incarnation takes a special form in the events of Jesus. Chapter 5 explores how God was present in bodily form in the life of Jesus. The Bible focuses on Jesus in the gospels, but Christians have understood many other biblical texts as talking about God's incarnation in Christ, so the chapter will examine a wide variety of biblical texts to understand God's incarnation in Jesus.

Incarnation does not stop with the birth of Jesus. Chapter 6 discusses the ways that Jesus' life and ministry were embodied. What can we learn about God's physical presence through seeing how Jesus carried out an embodied ministry?

Christian tradition and theology claim that God was born in Jesus and took on human flesh in this act of incarnation, but being human and having a body means more than birth. It also means death. For Jesus, death was the crucifixion. Chapter 7 looks at the embodiment of death in God's incarnation along with the biblical passages about the resurrection.

Chapter 8 concludes the book by addressing how God is incarnate after Jesus. God took a body in Jesus, and the early church proclaimed that the church itself was the body of Christ, in which God remains incarnate in the world then and now. God's incarnation began before Jesus and continues after Jesus through the life and activity of the church of Jesus' followers. God is present still.

1

WHEN GOD WALKED AMONG US

A day—a moment—can make all the difference in the world. With some of my best friends, I can remember the moment we first met. Someone sat next to me on the bus, and we struck up a conversation. I caught someone's eye across the room, then went over and introduced myself. Maybe another friend introduced us to each other. As years go by and friendships bloom, those early moments become special treasures, remembered often and always with great warmth and fondness.

Of course, some people I knew for years before we became friends. Maybe I can't remember the first e-mail that we exchanged years ago. The relationship began as business, but at some point there was a lull in the conversation and things turned personal, more by accident than by intention. After we realized we had more in common than we thought, we could never quite remember those earlier times when we knew each other but weren't yet friends.

Most friendships and relationships are a combination. There are special moments worth remembering for a lifetime, yet the relationship is constantly nurtured by a bounty of forgotten accidental instants. No relationship stays the same as those first moments, whether the beginnings are magical or much more mundane.

When relationships end, sometimes I can trace just where things went wrong. There was a word or deed that wounded and seemed never to go away or a sudden revelation that things would never be the same or that this was not the person I had long thought. More often, it's hard to tell. Relationships can come and go; they live and die to rhythms we do not quite hear clearly.

In some of my friendships, I wonder where things will go. Will we still be friends in ten years or in a half century? Will we retire to the same place, or will life's events take us far apart? But some relationships seem so secure that we cannot imagine that they will ever end.

Our relationship with God is the same in so many ways. We live life with God, always trying to get to know God better, striving to find stronger ways of relating, and building the relationship through time together. We talk together, share the stories of our lives through prayer and scripture, and celebrate together the joys and pains of our daily existence. We point to some moments as better than others, and some moments are truly life-changing. Sometimes, things do not go well and we hardly know what to say to each other—or we say things that will come back to haunt us. The Bible makes the astonishing claim that God is in relationship with us. Over and over again, the Bible tells of how God seeks us out and stays with us through all the changes of life that would drive lesser friendships apart. Humanity's relationship with God is enduring—both because we keep searching for God and because God keeps seeking to be in relationship with us.

In the Bible, God's relationship with humanity is incarnate. In other words, it is an embodied relationship like all of our human friendships and loves.[1] This is not just a mystical connection; God is not like a child's pretend friend. The Bible shows us a God who is active and present, who takes a real concern with these relationships

---

[1]For an introduction to the concept of embodiment in theology, see Anne Bathurst Gilson, "Embodiment," in Letty M. Russell and J. Shannon Clarkson, eds., *Dictionary of Feminist Theologies* (Louisville: Westminster John Knox Press, 1996), 82–83.

and makes real emotional investments in friendships with people, and who lives with us body and soul.

Some will say that these are merely "stories," somehow not quite as true as philosophical and theological arguments about the nature of God. But in a sense, the stories are all we have.[2] Although people have religious experiences, such events pass quickly and then become stories, or else they are forgotten. Stories shape our lives, or at least the stories form our interpretation of what our lives mean, especially the ultimate meaning of religion, faith, and life with God.

From the beginning of the Old Testament through the end of the New Testament, the God of the Bible is physically present and walks around in a body much like ours. To be sure, sometimes God is closer than others, and there are times when people cannot see God. But God throughout scripture relates to us humans as an incarnate, embodied being.

This can be a surprising thing to discover, because much of the church's tradition has emphasized God's distance from us. The doctrine of God's transcendence states that God is very different from us. Consider this hymn:

Immortal, invisible, God only wise,
In light inaccessible hid from our eyes,
Most blessed, most glorious, the Ancient of Days,
Almighty, victorious, thy great name we praise.

Unresting, unhasting, and silent as light,
Nor wanting, nor wasting, thou rulest in might;
Thy justice like mountains high soaring above
Thy clouds which are fountains of goodness and love.[3]

Hymns like this echo the insistence of so much theology that places God far away from us. God is immortal and invisible—completely unlike human beings and outside the range of what humans have ever experienced, since we have never known any being who is immortal or invisible. God is inaccessible, and the only metaphors for God's activity are massive formations of nature like mountains

---

[2]This is increasingly realized by theologians. For an atypical example, see Mark C. Taylor, *Erring: A Postmodern A/Theology* (Chicago: University of Chicago Press, 1984), 65, which sees incarnation as the center of the story in traditional Christianity.

[3]"Immortal, Invisible, God Only Wise," words by Walter Chalmers Smith (1867), alt., in *Chalice Hymnal* (St. Louis: Chalice Press, 1995), no. 66, vv. 1–2.

and clouds that are literally far over our heads. We humans tire easily, are clumsy, rush around in frequent ineffectiveness, experience lack and insufficiency; these are the things of human life that we live each day, but the hymn insists that God is completely unlike all of these things.

But the Bible paints a picture of God very different from this. God is not a completely alien being who shares nothing in common with weak, frail humans and whose feet (if God even has feet!) never touch the same earth that we walk. In fact, the Bible insists from the first to the last of its pages that God has a body.

At the Start

The Bible begins in Genesis 1 with God's creating everything. God had to start from scratch. God had earth, water, and wind, but none of them had any shape or form. Not even God could see how they all fit together, so first God lit up the world in order to see. Then God started to divide things, by putting waters, skies, and soil into separate piles. The first verses of Genesis 1 sound as if God was working on a massive workbench to create something special by hand. Of course, it all happened on a cosmic scale, far beyond the human. God is massive, with a gigantic body.[4]

Yet even the grandeur of the Bible's beginning, when God is huge and stands big enough to straddle worlds and separate out the land from the seas, already hints that God's body is not too different from ours.

> Then God said, "Let us make humankind in our image, according to our likeness; and let them have dominion over the fish of the sea, and over the birds of the air, and over the cattle, and over all the wild animals of the earth, and over every creeping thing that creeps upon the earth." (Gen. 1:26)

God creates humans to match God. We have the same likeness and the same image. Humans interact with nature just like God, reaching into the sea, the air, and the earth. We usually concentrate on how this means that God made us in good shape, according to God's own image. But it also tells us something about God because God's shape

---

[4]For a vivid and graphic discussion of the Old Testament and ancient Judaism's description of God's huge body, see Stephen D. Moore, *God's Gym: Divine Male Bodies of the Bible* (New York: Routledge, 1996), especially 73–138.

is like our shape. God's body is like our body; our own bodies are both the proof and the reflection of God's flesh.

The second chapter of Genesis depicts God on a more human scale. God made humans by hand, by kneeling down in the mud along a riverbank in a special garden, working with God's own hands, and blowing air into the human's nostrils (Gen. 2:7). Then, God stayed in the garden and showed Adam around. After God made Eve, the three of them would see each other when God would come to walk in the garden in the afternoons (Gen. 3:8). God had a body and walked among humans, and no one in Genesis seems to think that this is strange at all.[5]

At the beginning of the Bible, God is literally present. This is not the God who lives only in highest heaven. God lives in a garden on a hill, takes walks in the early evening, and chats with friends along the way. God is incarnate.

Of course, the Bible has a variety of other images of God, but God's body lingers throughout the text. When God is far away, it feels as though God is missing, or that God has left the people behind—because there is the constant sense that God was here in our midst, and God could be here again.

Throughout scripture, the memory returns. Israel knows that God was once in its midst in body. The prophet Hosea tells of this kind of memory:

When Israel was a child, I loved him,
    And out of Egypt I called my son.
    ....

Yet it was I who taught Ephraim to walk,

    I took them up in my arms;
    But they did not know that I healed them.
I led them with cords of human kindness,
    With bands of love.
I was to them like those
    Who lift infants to their cheeks.
    I bent down to them and fed them.
                (Hos. 11:1, 3–4)

---

[5]This is in sharp contrast to other ancient religions that told stories of how their gods fought in the heavens or of how a dead god's body became a whole island or continent.

God reminisces about those old days when God and Israel were together physically. They touched each other and held each other. God was a parent with a deep, abiding, and thoroughly physical love for a child. God taught Ephraim (another term for God's people) to walk, holding them by hand and stooping over while the baby took its first steps and grew into being a toddler. When the baby fell and skinned a knee, God picked the baby up in God's own arms to comfort and soothe. The comfort was physical; it was embodied. As the memory continues, it becomes even more palpable and sensuous. God is like a nurse to the baby Israel, lifting the little one up and bending over enough to let the child suck at God's breast. God feeds the child with God's own body.

We cannot imagine a God more embodied and more incarnate than this. God lived in our midst, shared a garden with us, took us by the hand, fed us from the breast, held us when we cried, patched up our skinned knees, and comforted our bruised hearts. This is God the way we remember, the way we long for God to be.

Hosea claims that God remembers. In this prophetic vision, God wants the sense of touch once more. The memory of when God could touch us in the flesh lingers in God's mind, not just in the mind of God's people, and the memory drives God onward.

God was incarnate at the start in Genesis' beginning and in the hints of memory in the midst of scripture. Our God knows how to be in a body; God began the relationship with humans that way, and God remembers those days fondly, no matter what else has happened in the meantime. We do not see God in the flesh these days. Many of the writers of the Bible did not claim to see God in the flesh in their day either. Yet they remembered the incarnate God, and they were assured that God remembered too. In that enduring memory is more than reminiscence, more than mere nostalgia. There are also the hope of a future and a certainty that God's embodiment did not end at Eden.

At the End

When the Bible envisions what things will be like at the end of time, that vision again shows God incarnate in flesh like ours.

Ezekiel struggled amid a changing world. He grew up in a priestly family at a time when Judah's monarchy was weak. He expected to become a priest like his father and take on the ancestral responsibilities for serving God in the temple. But the politics of the era were tenuous at best. By the time Ezekiel was old enough to be a priest, he and thousands of others were captured and deported to the land of Babylonia, where they would be slaves to a vast empire, whether as farm workers, as local supervisors, or as advisers to the emperor.

When Ezekiel looked into the future, he was shortsighted. He was looking for survival for himself, his family, his people, and his God, whom he had wanted to serve in the temple. The book of Ezekiel records his prophetic attempts to envision a future of survival for those around him. For Ezekiel, the end of the world was at hand. He had already lived through the end of his life as he had known it, and he wondered what would happen next. Would it be possible for life to go on in an unfamiliar land, without the temple where God lived, without the way of life that had meant the whole world to him?

Ezekiel's world was a mess, but the world that he saw in his visions of God's future was anything but messy. He envisioned a world that had order—a rigid, meticulous order. Ezekiel 40—48 details this vision of an orderly world. Ezekiel sees the lands of Israel and Judah re-divided and re-organized. Every tribe has its own space, exactly the same size and shape as the others. God has provided equally for all of God's people; there is no favoritism of geography in Ezekiel's vision of the future that God brings. In the visions, Ezekiel is often accompanied by a man with measuring-tape in his hands; the man measures everything in sight to make sure that it is all just right. Such is the care with which God constructs this future new world; every measurement is important, and God sends messengers to double-check everything.

At the center of the new land is a new city. This city has room for the priests to live in its midst (Ezek. 48:10–14), but the city as a whole is a city where all people can meet. Everyone is jointly responsible for growing food there, and everyone together partakes of what they grow (vv. 15–20). Also in this city is God's new temple, where God lives.

> I heard someone speaking to me out of the temple. He said
> to me: Mortal, this is the place of my throne and the place
> for the soles of my feet, where I will reside among the people
> of Israel forever. (Ezek. 43:6b–7a)

The priests live on one side of God's temple, and the public area of the city is on the other side (Ezek. 45). In this city, everyone lives side by side.

In this grand vision of God's future, God is once more physically present. Ezekiel watches God moving into the temple, and God even says that it is the place for the soles of God's feet. God lives there both body and soul. Ezekiel asserts that God is not absent forever, even if God seems to be gone at the moment. God will once more be among us in body, and when God comes back, God will live in our midst. In this vision, God lives just down the street from the people. Not even the priests separate God from the people. Anyone at the marketplace can see God's house and might just catch a glimpse of God out for a stroll or out in the garden in the cool of the day—just as the first people saw God in the flesh in the garden called Eden.

Not only is God physically present and right next door to all the people, but Ezekiel even renames the city. The last words of his vision are the city's new name, "Yahweh is there" (Ezek. 48:35, author's translation). Anyone who even talks about the city will know that it is where God lives, and that God is there in body.

A New Earth

At the Bible's end, God once more returns to earth to live among people. The Bible, arranged as it now is from Genesis to Revelation, moves full circle from when God walked among humans to when God returns to dwell among us again.

The book of Revelation tells a cosmic story about struggle between God and the forces of evil in heaven and earth. By the end of the book, horrible tribulations have come and gone on earth, and God has been proven victorious once more; the safety of God's people is again assured, and God's enemies are removed forever. In chapter 21, all of life starts over. The narrator announces the arrival of a new heaven and a new earth; everything that had been has passed away, and the old earth is no more. The book tells that a new Jerusalem is coming down from heaven, a brand new city as a gift from God. Just as Ezekiel longed for a new city that could create and symbolize a new way of life for God and God's people, the book of Revelation culminates in this vision of a new city that is God's gift to bring a new kind of life. This new Jerusalem comes to the new earth, but the biggest surprise is not the vastness of this cosmic scene, but instead an announcement from a heavenly voice.

And I heard a loud voice from the throne saying,
"See, the home of God is among mortals.

God will dwell with them as their God;
They will be God's peoples,
And the very God will be with them.
God will wipe every tear from their eyes.
Death will be no more;
Mourning and crying and pain will be no more,
For the first things have passed away."
And the one who was seated on the throne said, "See, I
      am making all things new." (Rev. 21:3–5a)

In this striking vision, the author of Revelation weaves together images from earlier parts of the Bible. In the Old Testament, the book of Isaiah had envisioned a time when God would "swallow up death forever" (Isa. 25:7) and "wipe away the tears from all faces" (Isa. 25:8). Other voices from Isaiah speak of the newness that Revelation envisions: "Do not remember the former things, or consider the things of old. I am about to do a new thing" (Isa. 43:18–19a). This prophetic tradition emphasized God's continuing creativity and God's constant desire to do new things. There are even prophetic visions of new creation, in which God says,

For I am about to create new heavens
and a new earth;
the former things shall not be remembered
or come to mind.
But be glad and rejoice forever
in what I am creating;
for I am about to create Jerusalem as a joy,
and its people as a delight.
I will rejoice in Jerusalem,
and delight in my people;
no more shall the sound of weeping be heard in it,
or the cry of distress. (Isa. 65:17–19)

These visions from the book of Isaiah tell of new cities, of the removal of death and mourning, and of God's activity in wiping tears from all eyes. The words of Isaiah were well known in the early Christian communities. Before Revelation echoed these cries of newness, Paul had used the same scriptural texts in one of his letters, when he wrote that "if anyone is in Christ, there is a new creation: everything old has passed away; see, everything has become new!" (2 Cor. 5:17).

God acts not only on a cosmic level (ending the processes of death within human existence) but also in deeply personal, embodied ways, such as wiping away tears from people's eyes.

Isaiah envisioned a God who would arrive in person, in the flesh, and wipe away tears from all eyes. But Revelation takes things one step further, echoing Ezekiel. The voice makes a startling claim: "The home of God is among mortals." God sets up a new home on the same streets of the city where all of God's people live. God roams the streets. God is not shut inside the temple because in this vision of God's future, there is no temple at all.

> I saw no temple in the city, for its temple is the Lord God the Almighty and the Lamb. And the city has no need of sun or moon to shine on it, for the glory of God is its light, and its lamp is the Lamb. The nations will walk by its light, and the kings of the earth will bring their glory into it. Its gates will never be shut by day—and there will be no night there. (Rev. 21:22–25)

God is embodied and is light itself. God lives and dwells in the city itself, in the very same bodily way that the people live and dwell in the city. But at the same time, God is present in ways that human bodies are not, with the pervasive presence of light. God is everywhere, and in God's light there will never again be darkness or night. God's presence is human, embodied, and touchable—and God's presence is much more.

Even though the whole world is in flux, even though the early church faced horrors of oppression, even though the heavens and the earth will pass away, God's physical, incarnate presence will endure. God may be made of pure light that overpowers the sun, but the vision also speaks of God as the one who wipes away the tears of each person who cries. God touches each person in mourning individually, one-on-one, face-to-face.

In Between

Moses

The Bible from Genesis to Ezekiel to Revelation tells of God's physical presence at the beginning and end of time. Incarnation is something that God does at the edges of history. In some ways, this is easy to believe for us because it allows us to have faith in God's real presence but pushes the experience of actually seeing and touching God to the distant past or the distant future. The fact of God's incarnation can be a matter of belief, but it does not come close to us or literally touch us. However, the Bible also tells stories of people who met God and who saw God face-to-embodied-face. These people experienced God's incarnation in the midst of regular life, not in the distant past or inaccessible future.

Moses offers an amazing story of a man who saw God face-to-face. The story of Moses covers the books of Exodus through Deuteronomy. When God's people, the Hebrews, were living in Egypt, they became slaves there. Moses was a Hebrew man who grew up in the Egyptian Pharaoh's royal court, and he became the leader whom God would use to bring God's people out of Egyptian slavery and into the wilderness, from which they would one day enter a promised land. While Moses was leading the Hebrew people, God also used him to explain God's law to the people, and so the tradition remembers Moses as liberator, leader, and lawgiver.

The story of Moses sounds grandiose. Certainly, the Bible depicts him as a great man and a hero of faith. But he was also a man caught in the middle of circumstances beyond his control.

His story begins as an infant discarded by his Hebrew mother and left to float downstream in a makeshift raft, where he was discovered and taken home by one of the women who found him. This woman happened to be the daughter of the Pharaoh, the emperor of Egypt. Moses then grew up in royal surroundings, but he developed an awareness that his family and his people were different from each other. He was caught in the middle between slavery and royal privilege. After forty years of life in Pharaoh's court, he rebelled and gave it all up, settling in the wilderness and living as a shepherd until he was eighty years old. Those must have been difficult years of hard work to care for the sheep and eke out a living from Egyptian rock and sand. It was then that God called to him, and Moses became God's chosen leader to bring all of God's chosen people out of slavery. Moses had lived half his life in the court and half in the rugged wilderness; he was a creature of both worlds, and there in the middle of these two cultures God found him.

Moses went as God's speaker to Pharaoh, who rejected God's plea to let the people out of slavery and to allow the Hebrews a chance to worship God elsewhere in peace. Moses never thought of himself as an effective speaker, and so he tried to convince God that he was the wrong person for the job. Instead, God told Moses to take along his brother Aaron, who was a good public speaker. Moses then complained that he needed proof to take to Pharaoh. He said he needed some sort of sign or miracle so that the Egyptian rulers would believe that his claim to represent God was legitimate. God gave Moses a staff as proof. The staff did two miraculous things: when tossed down, it became a poisonous snake, and when picked up, it turned back to a staff. That left Moses with the jobs of dealing with God, trying to convince a hostile Pharaoh, and now also picking up an angry, poisonous snake so that it would turn into a staff again. Moses was surrounded by problematic people and situations, from God's unwillingness to let Moses out of this unpleasant situation, to the Pharaoh's stubbornness and anger, to the inability to speak well, to the unwanted task of snake-handling.

Moses' life, in other words, was a rather normal one. He found himself caught between competing interests. Everyone wanted him to do certain things, and he had to make tough choices in his life. Even when he was able to get the help that he had requested, it threatened to turn on him and bite him. His helpers were few and far between, and he even had to do the thinking for his brother.

When Moses and the people left Egypt, he was their leader, but that was hardly a comfortable position. They complained to him and worked against his plans whenever he turned his back. They blamed him for their problems. He was still caught in the middle between God and people who did not want to listen. He had hopes and dreams, but they were dashed against the daily realities of everyone's conflicting whims. In the end, he died without reaching his goal; he never entered the land that God had promised to him and to everyone else.

When Moses needed a sign from God to get his attention and to change the path of his life in dramatic fashion, Moses saw a miraculously burning bush; he did not see God incarnate. When Moses needed signs to prove to Pharaoh that God had sent him to lead the people out of slavery, God sent Moses a magical staff, but God did not show God's body to Moses. At the great moments of Moses' transformation into a religious leader and at the miraculous times that Moses argued against the powers of the world and performed great deeds to bring God's people to salvation, God's incarnation was not apparent. Instead, Moses saw God's body only at a time of discouragement and depression late in life.

In the midst of this life of living in the middle, Moses saw God in the flesh.[6] Moses asked to see God face-to-face, but God said that it would not be allowed. Instead, God offered to let Moses see the rest of God's body.

> "I will make all my goodness pass before you, and will proclaim before you the name, 'The LORD'; and I will be gracious to whom I will be gracious, and will show mercy on whom I will show mercy. But," God said, "you cannot see my face; for no one shall see me and live." And the LORD continued, "See, there is a place by me where you shall stand on the rock; and while my glory passes by I will put you in a cleft of the rock, and I will cover you with my hand until I have passed by; then I will take away my hand, and you shall see my back; but my face shall not be seen." (Exod. 33:19–23)

In this way, Moses could see God's body. He would not see God's face, but he would see God's hand and backside, and he would know the glory of God.

The idea of God incarnate and physically present is not something that the Bible limits to its beginning and end, nor to the start and climax of human history. God's body is present not only at those margins of time, but also in the middle of God's activity in the world. Moses was not a common man, but he was caught in the middle of daily life in the same ways that people always are. His opportunity to see God's body is part of the Bible's insistence that God is incarnate in all times and places. Not everyone sees God's body, and even those who do see God's body do not see all of it. But the embodied nature of God is assumed throughout the Old Testament. God is not a disembodied spirit, but a creature of flesh and blood. Moses does not discuss what God's body looks like, but after he sees God in the flesh, Moses is never the same again. There is a reality to God, a physical presence, that is easy for people to forget and ignore. In the times between the beginning and end of history, God seems to be shy and

---

[6]Sallie McFague, *The Body of God: An Ecological Theology* (Minneapolis: Fortress Press, 1993), 131–36, offers a "meditation" on this passage, commenting on the divine back as a way of rethinking God's distance and presence.

rarely appears in flesh. But God remains embodied, and at times God's body appears in the middle of human existence in ways that always transform.

Abraham and Sarah

When God appears to the great leaders of the faith, such as Moses, the sight of God's body within the Old Testament text seems almost unsurprising. After all, Moses had spoken with God many times, and God clearly favored Moses with a special relationship that God affords to few. But God appears in flesh to others besides those who are already famous.

Besides Moses, one of the most prominent characters of the Old Testament is Abraham. He was the head of the family that made the move from Mesopotamia to the land that would become known as Israel, so in his stories the readers of the Old Testament first enter the main stage for the rest of the Old Testament's narratives. But at the story's beginning, Abraham was simply a man named Abram (his name was changed later) living in Mesopotamia in an average city, leading an average life. Then, God sent Abram a message, telling him to move with his family and to start life over in a brand new place. This began the journey that Abram and God would take together.

When God first spoke to Abram (Gen. 12:1–3), the message was direct, and Abram obeyed. The book of Genesis does not provide details about how Abram saw or heard God. But this initial instruction was hardly the last time that God and Abram spoke. Over time, their interactions became more complex. Their next interaction comes in a series of Abram's dreams (Gen. 15:1–21). This time, Abram speaks back to God and asks questions, and God then explains. In fact, God develops signs for Abram to see, and God offers Abram a further promise (vv. 18–21). No longer is their relationship one only of directions and instructions; they have now progressed to questions, answers, and promises.

When Abram was ninety-nine years old, God appeared to him again (Gen. 17:1–22). This time, the text never says that the appearance was in a dream or a vision. It simply says that God appeared to Abram. At the end, God went up and away from him. The language suggests that this is the same as any embodied being speaking to another, not a mystical appearance of a spirit. During their conversation

God did almost all the speaking, and in the process, God renamed Abram as Abraham and his wife, Sarai, as Sarah.

In the very next chapter, God appeared to Abraham and Sarah both. This time, God brought two friends along, who did not speak during the conversation and who were not even present by the end. The text of Genesis 18 treats this whole scenario as if it was perfectly normal. Sarah even made breakfast for God and the other two beings, as if they were regular houseguests. Even though this may seem odd to readers today, it points to the theological sense that permeates the whole Old Testament—that it was perfectly normal to think of God as an embodied being who can appear to people in the middle of the day, showing up in the flesh to do normal activities such as eating breakfast.

In this encounter between God and Abraham, something else amazing happens. God announces plans to destroy Sodom, a neighboring town with a bad reputation. Abraham hears these plans and then argues with God. Although it is clear that God intends Sodom's destruction, Abraham asks if God will really do it.

> Then Abraham came near and said, "Will you indeed sweep away the righteous with the wicked? Suppose there are fifty righteous within the city; will you then sweep away the place and not forgive it for the fifty righteous who are in it? Far be it from you to do such a thing, to slay the righteous with the wicked, so that the righteous fare as the wicked! Far be that from you! Shall not the Judge of all the earth do what is just?" (Gen. 18:23–25)

Abraham ventures to argue with God. He questions the wisdom and appropriateness of God's own stated intentions. Abraham's argument is based on the nature of God as judge and as the righteous, just one; he suggests that God would violate God's own nature were God to go through with these plans for destruction.

Part of embodied life is disagreement. Because we are each different, separate individuals, we have different perspectives on life. We each see things that others do not, and sometimes other people see us more accurately than we see ourselves. In the biblical text, Abraham seems to more clearly state who God is than God realizes. Thus, they disagree about the nature and proper actions of God—and then God agrees with Abraham.

> And the LORD said, "If I find at Sodom fifty righteous in the
> city, I will forgive the whole place for their sake." (Gen. 18:26)

God admits that Abraham is right, and God promises to make a change in plans, adjusting for Abraham's own argument. But God still intends to destroy Sodom, so Abraham presses on. Abraham keeps arguing with God, negotiating God from fifty to forty-five to forty. Abraham thinks that God is wrong to destroy the city of Sodom. The argument continues with the same results; Abraham keeps lowering the number, and God keeps agreeing to Abraham's argument. Eventually, they reach the number of ten. If ten righteous are found, God will not destroy the city.

In the end, six righteous people were found in Sodom that God's messengers thought were worth saving: Lot's family (Gen. 19). One wonders why Abraham did not continue the argument with God. If God would have agreed to reducing the number once more to five, the messengers would have found one more person than the number needed to save the city. Would this have been more true to God's own character, to save a city for the sake of a few? It seems that Abraham would have thought so.

This story from Genesis portrays God as one whose mind might well be changed. Abraham argues with God over the future of Sodom. The relationship between them has the character of give-and-take relationships among people. Abraham even helps God to act more like God. Despite the traditional theological assertions of God's unchangeability, it seems quite possible that Abraham is persuading God toward more appropriate action. These pictures of God disturb the reader because they go against the traditional theological portrayals of God as beyond the human realm, but they reflect the Bible's typical notions about God. God is incarnate, and because God is in the flesh, God acts as other embodied beings do—and this requires interaction with others.

Hagar

Abraham's story stretches across a large part of the middle of the book of Genesis. He is usually accompanied by his wife, Sarah, who was also his half-sister. Their relationship was troubled by Abraham's own denials of their marriage and by the fact that for many years (perhaps the first fifty years of their time together) they had no children—despite the fact that God had appeared to Abraham and had repeatedly promised that they would have numerous children.

Abram first adopted Eliezer (Gen. 15:2), but this did not stop the desire. Later, Abram impregnated Hagar, an Egyptian slave in their household who was Sarai's personal maid.

From the first moment that Sarai knew of Hagar's pregnancy, there were problems within the household. Sarai sent Hagar away, out into the wilderness; Abram agreed with this idea. There in the desert, an angel of God met Hagar, gave her water to drink, and sent her back to Abram and Sarai. Hagar, however, thought that she had seen God, not just an angel. She even named God there as El–roi, the God I have seen (Gen. 16:13). Translators have frequently rendered this as "God of seeing" or "God who sees," even though Hagar explained what she meant: "Have I really seen God and remained alive?" Hagar thought that she saw God.

The child was a boy, named Ishmael. But even this precious baby boy was not enough for Abram and Sarai, and in just a few years, Sarah became pregnant with Isaac. Sarah wanted Hagar and Ishmael removed. Abraham banished Hagar and Ishmael and sent them off to the wilderness to fend for themselves in a harsh world that had few opportunities for a former slave and her unclaimed toddler.

Abraham had given his lover and his son only a bit of bread and a single skin of water, and in the desert wilderness these provisions were soon gone. Thirst set in, and death seemed sure to follow quickly. When their end seemed certain, Hagar found a bush for shade and set Ishmael underneath it; then Hagar went a little ways away, praying that God would not make her watch her only son die.

The timing of the story only makes Abraham and Sarah's cruelty all the more apparent. The story begins with the statement "Abraham made a great feast on the day that Isaac was weaned" (Gen. 21:8). A party is going on, with more good food than one can imagine. Isaac is the center of the celebration. At the same time, Ishmael is cast out and left to die with not enough food and not enough water. Abraham has more than enough to raise many sons—in fact, God kept promising that Abraham's sons would be more numerous than he could count—but Abraham does not seem to be able to count any higher than one. One son is all that he can handle, all that he wants, and all that he will allow. He sends Ishmael and Hagar to their deaths rather than let his own love be multiplied.

When the story seems determined to become another numbing tale of a disadvantaged woman and boy forgotten by the powerful and privileged, God appears.

> Then God opened her eyes and she saw a well of water. She went, and filled the skin with water, and gave the boy a drink. God was with the boy, and he grew up; he lived in the wilderness, and became an expert in the bow. (Gen. 21:19–20)

This part of the story is so simple, so anticlimactic, that it is easy to ignore or to downplay or to miss the incarnation of God. If we as readers are used to thinking of God as a disembodied spirit who appears only through visions, that may be all we read here. But if we have learned to read God's body when it appears, then we will notice that God is physically present with Hagar and Ishmael. God is more present than we have known, and the Bible sees God's body in far more places than most of our own hymns and theologies have dared to dream.

God opens her eyes. In other parts of the Bible, God appears in the flesh to wipe the tears away from the eyes of those who mourn. In the same way, God appears to Hagar, whose eyes are spending her body's last water to cry over the death of her only son. God wipes away Hagar's tears with the same tenderness and compassion with which God touches the mourners in Isaiah and Revelation.

Of course, God does much more than stop the crying. God deals with the problems that caused the mourning. Hagar's son is not yet dead, and God acts to stop the death. God points to a nearby well, and with the eyes that God's touch opened, Hagar sees the well and draws from it the water that will keep her boy alive. God's touch, combined with Hagar's action, brings life.

Once Hagar and Ishmael have a source of water that is enough to keep them alive, God does not abandon them. Life itself is not the goal of God's activity in this story. Instead, God works toward a quality of life and a relationship that makes life worthwhile. God stays there in the wilderness. When the text says that "God was with the boy" while Ishmael was growing up in the desert, there is no reason to think of this merely as a disembodied, spiritual presence. Instead, it makes more sense within the context of ancient beliefs to envision that God moved in with Ishmael and Hagar. God lived with them in the flesh and stayed there to make sure that Ishmael grew up well.

God sought out this abandoned mother and child, and God in the flesh became family with them and parent to the boy. When the story relates the detail that Ishmael learned the bow, the natural conclusion is that God taught Ishmael this skill. God's continuing activity allows life, relationship, and a future.

All these claims are a reading of the text consistent with the ancient notion of an embodied God. Later interpretations that stressed God's transcendence and physical absence turned the stories into tales of God's spiritual assistance, but the biblical stories themselves consistently assume God's embodied physical presence. God saves people, dwells with them, and participates in their lives—and all of these are things that God does in the flesh.

God appears face-to-face, in the flesh, to live with common people like this Egyptian slave Hagar and her forgotten son. God's appearances are not limited to the wealthy, the powerful, or the elites of God's chosen people. Sometimes, in the midst of broken lives, shattered situations, and the evils done in the name of propriety, God appears in the flesh.

Psalm 23

The Hebrew Bible is full of the assured knowledge of a God who helps those whom other people have marginalized or victimized. The hurting and oppressed of the world, like Hagar, are those most likely to see God. In Psalm 23, one of the best-known psalms of the Bible, God appears as a shepherd. This portrayal is of course metaphorical; God is not a literal shepherd tending literal sheep, but instead acts with people in ways that are similar to the kinds of embodied care that shepherds provide for sheep. It is striking that so many of the images within this psalm are images of embodiment. God is not a lofty deity far removed from the human realm; instead, the poem praises God's most human, embodied acts. God finds water for the thirsting, provides guidance and safe paths for the feet, offers protection of rod and staff against marauding predators, cooks a meal and sets a table, touches the head with sweet perfumes, and offers a permanent house in which to live. In all these ways, God is physically present. The image of an embodied God is an image of comfort. God's nature is to care for others in embodied ways as an incarnate God. When God is seen in the flesh is when God is known as most caring.

Pushed to the Edges

The Bible tells stories of God's physical presence throughout, from its first pages to its last. But where do we see God most clearly?

Certainly the stories of Genesis depict a God who is at home in the world in very natural ways. When God walks in the garden in the cool of the afternoon, God's embodiment seems unexceptional. When cool breezes blow through Eden's heat, who wouldn't want to stroll through the meadows and forests of that beautiful place? God seems quite at home there and perfectly comfortable in sharing those physical joys of the body with Adam, Eve, and the animals who all live their embodied lives of the flesh along with God. But Eden seems a mystical, magical place to us; it is not much like our own daily lives at all. An embodied God who walks in Eden may be embodied but is hardly like one of us, because none of us walk in Eden.

When God appears in the flesh at the end of time, this too makes perfect sense to us. Whether in Isaiah's or Ezekiel's visions or in the book of Revelation, God makes a new world in which God's own physical presence is perfectly logical. When we see God incarnate in a new kind of world, freshly created, it doesn't surprise us to see God feeling once more at home there. With these texts in mind, it is tempting to think of the world as having once been God's home and in great need of re-creation so that God can once more walk our streets safely. Ezekiel gets a little provocative in the prophetic images of God living on streets like ours, settling into our neighborhoods. If the streets are made of gold (as in Revelation) or if all of the story happens on God's holy mountain (as in Isaiah), God's presence is sufficiently far away that God's body doesn't threaten us. Even though Ezekiel envisions God walking the same city streets we walk, they are not streets of gold; but neither are they the same streets we walk now. God's body comes into our midst only after the world changes to be utterly unlike the world we now know, a world where God seems all too absent. We do not see God's body in our daily life, and our own experience affects how we read the biblical text. It becomes easier to think of God as far away, for that is how we have learned to feel about God.

Even though we can be tempted to make sense of things this way, other biblical passages argue against it. God appears in the middle of history. God appears in average, everyday times and places. Certainly,

God appears to religious leaders like Moses. God reaches out to them and even shows them God's body, at least in part. But God does not appear to leaders in times of their glory. Instead, even the leaders see God at moments of despair while living on the edges of an unattainable promised land and struggling in the midst of rejection by an ungrateful, uncomprehending people. God appears to Hagar in the moment when death looms large, and God even chooses to stay with Hagar and her rejected son for years.

Our religious traditions and our theology direct us to think of God as far away, but the Bible tells these stories of God in flesh among us, walking in our midst. These biblical stories break down the differences that we construct between God who is absent in our daily lives and God who was present at the creation and who will be present at the very end when everything becomes something completely unlike anything we have ever known. Instead, the Bible suggests that God is in the flesh among people at times in the midst of living. We might see God more easily not at the moments when God acts with power, but at the moments of despair, at the moments of abandonment, and at the moments of alienation and rejection. God's body resides not at the beginning and end of history, but instead in the midst of life, especially when our lives are at the fringes and margins of society. Hagar meets God's body at the fringes of the desert wilderness; Moses sees God from a tiny cave in an inaccessible mountain; both of them find God as they stand at the edge of life and at the brink of despair. This may be where God's body is most easily found—and most naturally at home.[7]

The church's theology has presented us with an image of God as distant and as unlike humans, even as disembodied and uninterested in human realities. This pervades so many of contemporary theology's images of God, even those enshrined in hymns:

> To all, life thou givest, to both great and small;
> In all life thou livest, the true life of all;
> We blossom and flourish like leaves on the tree,
> And wither and perish, but naught changeth thee.[8]

---

[7]These understandings of God are closely related to ideas that have been called embodiment theologies or incarnational theologies, and parts of ecofeminist and liberation theologies as well.

[8]"Immortal, Invisible, God Only Wise," v. 3.

God does not quite seem to care about human life at all in this image. True, God is the one who grants life to all, but God is unchanging. Perhaps all of our lives from birth to death make as much impact on an unchangeable God as the life and death of a leaf makes on us humans. We may notice it, we may appreciate the beauty of spring and the grandeur of fall's colors as seen in that leaf, we may even pick up an occasional dead leaf to save and cherish, but we do not find ourselves personally involved with leaves that come and go each season in numbers we will never bother to count. Is God that far away from us?

Even the hymn hints that this perception of God as inaccessible cannot hold true:

> Thou reignest in glory; thou dwellest in light,
> Thine angels adore thee, all veiling their sight;
> All praises we render: O help us to see
> That only the splendor of light hideth thee.[9]

For the first time in this hymn, God becomes the subject of verbs that humans can do: God reigns and dwells. The hymn then turns to prayer, asking God to help us see the God that is hidden. No longer is God inaccessible; God is simply hidden, and the prayer holds out a hope that God may want us to seek, to find, and to see God. God is not so far away that God cannot be seen, nor is God the kind of incorporeal, disembodied being that cannot be seen. Throughout the Bible, there are stories and images of God in flesh, and this is a God whom we can see and touch.

---

[9]Ibid., v. 4.

2

SEEING GOD AMONG US

This embodied God is a being of passion and compassion. To say that God cares about people or cares for creation somehow falls short of the image of God presented in these biblical texts. God is much more involved than that. God yearns for people. God desires contact and real relationship. God makes choices and takes risks as part of living life with people. God wants to live next to us humans and will move heaven and earth themselves to make it happen. This embodied God is vibrant, alive, and powerful.

Through biblical texts and the worship of congregations, we gain the sense of a memory that we have seen God. At times in the past the personal experience of God's presence has seemed more real. But the daily routines of our lives make us feel distant from God, as if we are miles apart. We long for those days when we can see God face-to-face, or when in any way the experience of God's close presence will be more real than it is to us in these days. God seems so far away, and yet we desire to see God. The desire can be a powerful motivation for us; our longing for God's presence and for a chance to see God can push us into many actions. Like persons who walk along a crowded street and think they see a friend or relative or lover in the crowd, we can begin to think that we see God when God is not there.

In human relationships across distances or in the midst of cyberspace, we experience a combination of physical presence and absence. We assume that the other has a body, and we long to see and touch our loved ones, whether again or for the first time. But we daily experience an absence of presence, and this fuels our desire. We are left without the touch, only with the trace of words echoed across telephone lines, glowing upon computer screens, or replayed in our memories.

Is God still present even when not visible? When we fail to see and touch God or to experience God as present in physical body on a daily basis, are we mistaken, and is God really here? Such questions are quandaries at the boundaries of faith.[1] We experience our own human longing for God. The perception of a loved one's absence can bring about powerful motivations. This may include deep acts of devotion and innovative ways to keep relationships vibrant and alive in the midst of absence, but it may also involve activity that is damaging, motivated by the same desire. With great fervency we search for God, and find the traces and mirrors of God in many places, but sometimes we start to see God where God is not present. Such is always the result when we humans try to see the invisible.

Seeing the Invisible

Christian belief resides in the awkward spaces between incarnation and invisibility. We affirm the physical, embodied presence of a God that we do not now see. Yet we long to see the invisible God, whom we are convinced dwelled among us in the flesh. The writer of the New Testament letter called 1 John reflected on the situation in this way:

> See what love the Father has given us, that we should be called children of God; and that is what we are. The reason that the world does not know us is that it did not know God. Beloved, we are God's children now; what we will be has not

---

[1] See David W. Odell-Scott, *A Post-Patriarchal Christology*, American Academy of Religion Academy Series 78 (Atlanta: Scholars Press, 1991), 82: "The doctrine of the incarnation involves that which is absent, a trace which is erased."

yet been revealed. What we do know is this: when God is revealed, we will be like God, for we will see God as God is. (1 John 3:1–2)

This writer draws a parallel between the world that does not see or know God and the fact that we believers ourselves are not fully seen or known. Someday it will all be clear to everyone, and then it will be seen that God and people look alike. As in many relationships, the longer we are together, the more alike we look. When we see God, then we will truly see ourselves for the first time. This short piece from near the end of the New Testament provides two important clues as we struggle to understand what happens when humans seek to see God. First, there may be problems in our own vision. Second, there is a resemblance between God and people.

We cannot see God in our daily lives; we see no evidence that God is an embodied being physically present in this world. Incarnation remains unprovable and in many cases unbelievable; at least, God's embodiment is invisible. Yet it may well be that this lack of vision is not God's fault. Instead, it may be the result of a human inability or at least a difficulty in perceiving the presence of God in our midst. The lack of sight does not then suggest that God does not exist, but instead suggests that our vision is inadequate to see truly. Almost by definition, it may be impossible to tell which of these is the case. In other words, we may never know why we do not see God around us, whether it is because God is absent or because we have a certain selective blindness. This indeterminacy and uncertainty should not be surprising to believers; after all, the letter to the Hebrews defined faith as "the assurance of things hoped for, the conviction of things not seen" (Heb. 11:1). Our lack of vision is precisely what enables us to have faith because otherwise we would have sight instead.

At the same time, recognizing our peculiar lack of vision enables us to begin to notice what else we are not seeing. As the writer called John notes, "what we will be has not yet been revealed" (1 John 3:2). Perhaps there is a connection here; perhaps we fail to see God for the same reason we fail to see ourselves.

Thus, the second clue is that we are created in God's image. We share bodies like God's body, and God appears—when we can see God—in human flesh. It is as if looking at God and looking in a mirror are the same thing because of this resemblance. In some ways, the best way to see God is to stare at each other. In each other, we see bodies in God's image. We experience care from one who teaches us to love. Here we catch glimpses of God, shrouded in our own flesh, embodied in people like us.

The Blind Leading the Blind

As we strive to see God, we look at each other. Because God tries to care for us through other people and through human activity, and because God has created us to be caring and productive even as God is, this strategy often works. One of the best examples comes from early in Moses' time during the journey of the Hebrew people in the wilderness.

As with any group of people, there was not harmony. When conflicts arose, Moses would listen to all sides and would offer advice and would discern paths to justice for those affected. In this way, God's care for the people would become visible through Moses' actions.

But the group was large, and Moses was only one person. It was not possible for him to address everyone's concerns. One day, his father-in-law, Jethro, the priest of Midian, offered advice to Moses (Exod. 18:13–24). Jethro suggested that Moses select and train others to do the same thing that Moses was doing. Then a number of persons could listen to each other's disputes and offer a word from God. Moses accepted this advice, and the Hebrew people gained from this practice of justice because it allowed people to hear God's voice and to sense God's presence (Num. 11:16–30).

The system embodied care for each other within the community of God's people. It became a way that people could hear God's voice even if they could not see God in the flesh. But often this isn't enough for us. We keep seeking ways to see God. The search is good, and the clues to God's presence and reality are visible throughout much of how people care for each other. But sometimes we can panic. We can be like children in a store, when for an instant a parent is no longer in view and suddenly life seems empty. The parent's absence becomes all-consuming, and the tendency to search can make the child wander away and even at times get into danger by following others who are not the parent. In similar panic, we become susceptible to mistaken visions, and our judgment is impaired. Not every human act is a manifestation of the image of God, and in our panic and sense of loss at God's absence, we can become disoriented and lost, sometimes accepting human institutions as embodiments of God when they are not.

In the story of ancient Israel, the people had a cultural memory of when God was more visible and more easily followable. When they were in the desert, the people could follow Moses, the leader whom God chose and who in most cases represented God's love and care for the people. The story also tells of other visible signs of God's presence, such as a pillar of cloud by day and of fire by night. The pillars first appeared just before God and Moses led the Hebrews across the Red Sea and into the wilderness (Exod. 13:21–22; 40:34–35; cf. Num. 9:15–23).

When God is present with the people in these visible ways, following becomes much easier. Hardly anyone gets lost if the signs are as big as the pillars of cloud and fire. But following God is not always that simple, and God's presence rarely takes such visible form. Without the cloud and fire, how can people decide which way to go? How can the community of God's people take shape? Without leadership, how will disputes be settled? Without authorized teachers, how will God's word and voice be heard? When God is less visible, the search for other ways to organize life intensifies, and the temptation to find other authority increases. The book of Deuteronomy begins to express this concern:

> When you have come into the land that the LORD your God is giving you, and have taken possession of it and settled in it, and you say, "I will set a king over me, like all the nations that are around me," you may indeed set over you a king whom the LORD your God will choose. (Deut. 17:14–15a)

This first mention of the possibility of a king ties it directly to the search to see God. The desire for a king begins when the people perceive an absence and when they start to look outside their own community. Their standard for right behavior is no longer the pillar, or the divinely chosen leader. Instead, they begin to think that they need to look like other nations. The image of God becomes less important than the image of worldly powers. God still insists on the right to choose the king, according to this passage, and Deuteronomy lists some of the problems that a king can create.

Human leadership is not bad in the Old Testament. In fact, the kingship is surprisingly ambiguous within the Bible. Many of the kings are praised for (at least some of) what they do: David, Solomon, Josiah, and Hezekiah, especially. But many passages resist the notion that a king would be good, even though most of the writers saw that the kingship was an unavoidable reality of Israel's history.

Samuel was a prophet and judge who brought the word of God to the people of Israel in the days before kings. When Samuel was old, many of the elders of the people of Israel came to him and asked that he appoint a king to succeed him, so that they could be like other nations (1 Sam. 8:4–6). Samuel clearly did not think that this was a good idea, and so he talked to God about it.

> The LORD said to Samuel, "Listen to the voice of the people in all that they say to you; for they have not rejected you, but they have rejected me from being king over them. Just as they have done to me, from the day I brought them up out of Egypt to this day, forsaking me and serving other gods, so also they are doing to you. Now then, listen to their voice; only—you shall solemnly warn them, and show them the ways of the king who shall reign over them." (1 Sam. 8:7–9)

"The ways of the king" are a sobering list of the realities of human leadership. Kings kidnap children or employ them in military service. The military machinery that kings require will affect the whole economy, and massive numbers of people will be needed as farmers and bakers to feed the war machine. Taxes will support not only the military but also all the court employees that surround the royal bureaucracy and the system of nobility that defines who is closest to the king. In the end, it is as if all the people are nothing but slaves of the king. The king's will begins as leadership, but it ends in oppression.

The book of 1 Samuel proclaimed clearly the dangers of kingship, but it also showed Samuel involved in anointing the first two kings of Israel: Saul (1 Sam. 9—10) and David (1 Sam. 16). These two men were of different families, dissimilar appearance, and conflicting temperaments. Each of them succeeded in some ways and failed in others. Yet God chose them both. In leadership, God's image becomes visible as the leaders are in partnership with God. But leaders do not perfectly reflect God.

We can find glimpses of God in each other. Through human institutions, people can care for each other to provide food, clothing, shelter, warmth, advice, justice, protection, security, community, hope, and faith. Human community and its leadership become ways that people of diminished visibility can see God in our midst. But idolatry is always close at hand. Instead of seeing community and leadership as reflections of God's image, we can mistakenly think that the human institutions are God, or that they completely, perfectly express the divine will.

Realizing that our own blindness—or God's absence—makes us unable to see God in the present, we turn to others, hoping for their vision. But the leaders are inevitably as blind to God as others are. It is inevitable because the lack of clear vision affects us all. To be certain, some see more clearly than others, and each may see a part of God that others miss. Together we may be able to see more of God than any one of us separately ever could. The goods of human community must not be dismissed, but neither should communities and their leaders be absolutized and idolized. Leaders are as blind as their followers; none see God clearly in these days when God is not visible in the flesh.

Such was the lesson of one of Jesus' parables:

> Can a blind person guide a blind person? Will not both fall into a pit? A disciple is not above the teacher, but everyone who is fully qualified will be like the teacher. (Luke 6:39b–40)

Human leaders are not better than human followers, nor are followers better than teachers. The gap between them fades quickly, even if bridging that gap may bring one closer to God's image. For leaders and followers alike, the pit is a real and continually present danger.

The Blind Seeking the Blind

Biblical texts are cautious about human leadership, likening it to enslavement and to the blind leading the blind. Although each person can see some part of God and catch a glimpse of God's image in looking at each other, none of us sees clearly and no one person's vision can be allowed to replace others' attempts to see. However, some of Jesus' parables offer a strikingly different vision of how to see God within the world.

Jesus talked about a time of judgment at the world's end, when those who were worthy of heaven would be separated from those who were deserving of eternal punishment. The king who would decide everyone's fate blessed the righteous because they had seen the king and had provided food, water, shelter, clothing, and comfort to the king. However, the righteous had no memory of doing these acts of divine compassion:

> Then the righteous will answer him, "Lord, when was it that we saw you hungry and gave you food, or thirsty and gave you something to drink? And when was it that we saw you a stranger and welcomed you, or naked and gave you clothing? And when was it that we saw you sick or in prison and visited you?"

> And the king will answer them, "Truly I tell you, just as you did it to one of the least of these who are members of my family, you did it to me." (Matt. 25:37–40)

In Jesus' vision, people see God not because they look to leaders, but instead because they recognize the needy in their midst. People who see human needs and respond with divine compassion are people who have seen God. To see God is to respond with one's body, for God is seen through the fleshly needs of real people, especially those people in the middle of suffering.

Jesus' parable about the king's judgment at the end of the world freely admitted that many people look at suffering in the world and fail to see therein the embodied presence of God. We resist thinking that we would be more like God if we were hungry, thirsty, homeless, naked, alone, or imprisoned. The parable haunts us, reminding us of God's presence in ways that we too often choose not to see.

Another of Jesus' parables makes the point, as well. Jesus told a story about a man traveling from Jerusalem to Jericho (Luke 10:25–37). Along the way, the man was mugged and beaten. The robbers left the man for dead along the roadside. When a priest walked by, the priest ignored the man. When a Levite walked by, the Levite ignored the man. Then a Samaritan (a person from a region that was disliked by many of the Jews in Jesus' audience because they thought that the Samaritans were wrong about their religion) walked along the same road, saw the man, and cared for him. The Samaritan took the beaten man to the city; made sure that he had shelter, food, and health care; and paid his bills while he healed. Jesus praised the

Samaritan in this story because he was the only one of the three who showed mercy to the man who had been robbed and beaten.

The story's three passersby see the same thing—a man left for dead at the side of the road. But they have different visions of what to do. Two of them ignore the man, and the third sees an opportunity to help. One of the reasons that this story can be so offensive is that the religious leaders did not see anything that they could or would do to help the man left for dead. The tenets of religion are not always helpful as we strive to see God or to live lives where others see God. The occasion of suffering and the opportunity to show compassion are places where God can be seen.

In this sense, we are not the blind leading the blind, for we do not lead each other. All of us, with our diminished ability to see God in the world and in the flesh, lack the capacity to show God to each other, to explain God's presence, or to seek God through our striving to see. However, we can seek each other, striving to reach and touch each other in the midst of our hurts, so that we can bind up the wounds that come to all who live embodied earthly lives. When we seek people as unseeing as we are ourselves, we find God's presence after all. If we do not wish to be like the blind leading the blind, perhaps we should be like the blind seeking the blind—to help each other and soothe each other, knowing that in the acts of care and in the shape of other uncertain faces will be found the image of God.

Ruth

One of the Old Testament's most beloved short stories is the book of Ruth. The story begins with a family beset by tragedy. In the midst of famine, a couple moved out of Israel to Moab, where they had two sons. But death struck the husband and then also the two sons. The woman considered her scant options and decided to go back to Israel to find family with whom she could live, and she told her daughters-in-law that they should go back to their own relatives too. One of them, Orpah, agreed. The other, Ruth, resisted. She insisted on staying with Naomi. The two of them walked to Israel, back to Naomi's distant past and a land that Ruth had never seen, where she could not speak the language or understand the customs.

According to Israelite custom, Naomi and Ruth were allowed to walk behind the harvesters who were picking grain, and they could pick up anything that the harvesters dropped and keep it for their own. Although this system meant difficult labor for little reward, it was Israel's own system of social support, and it allowed these women a chance to live. Ruth went to the fields every day and picked up dropped grain for her and her mother-in-law, Naomi, to eat.

This gleaning gave them enough to eat each day, but it was a short-term solution at best. Ruth could glean only as long as the harvest lasted, and eventually harvest season would be over. In the beginning of chapter 3, Naomi devised a plan that would give them a future. Naomi proposed a seduction. Ruth would clean herself up and put on her most attractive clothes. Then she would go to the part of town where all the men were at the end of their biggest party of the year. Ruth would wait until the town's richest man was drunk and would then go lie down with him when he went to bed. Whatever he suggested to do after that, Ruth would not say no. Through this seduction, Naomi hoped that Ruth would buy them a future.

The next morning, Boaz sent Ruth on her way before the dawn awoke the other men, and he sent her with as much grain as she could carry—enough for a few weeks, but hardly a long-term solution.

But the story does not end there. Boaz bought the entire estate of Naomi's deceased husband. The land would be worth something to a man like Boaz, who could afford the labor to make it productive. But Boaz's purchase also meant the purchase of the estate's responsibilities, and that included Naomi and Ruth. When Boaz bought the estate, he guaranteed a future for Naomi and Ruth. He married Ruth, and they parented a child before the elderly Boaz died.

The book's final scene presents all the roles as reversed. The women of the community pronounced that Ruth was worth more to Naomi than seven sons, even though Ruth was not a son at all and was not even really a daughter. Naomi, an elderly woman who had complained at the story's start that her childbearing years were long over, became the wet nurse for Ruth and Boaz's son. This son would inherit Boaz's estate, and he was in his flesh the legal guarantee for Naomi and Ruth's care, even though he was an infant who needed their daily care. The women of the community entered to perform the father's role of naming the son, who would one day be the ruler of the estate, and they named him Obed, which means "slave."

In all of this reversal, it would be hard for the boy to think of who was mother or father—Ruth who bore him? Naomi who nursed him, but who was a maternal grandmother and a paternal distant cousin? The women who named him? The man who fathered him but whom he would never meet? The entire situation was confusing at best. The relationships upon which normal society bases itself were all sundered and mixed around. Yet at the same time, the story ends with powerful acts of salvation. Whereas the characters of the story began a few chapters earlier with famine, death, and homelessness, they end the story with food and shelter, with new life, with possibility for future sustenance, and in rich relationship and harmony with the community. Salvation has come.

God works through those who are of much less influence and of little official standing at all. Even though leaders such as Moses and Abraham are means to see God at work in the world and to experience God's salvation at some points in time, the community of people who interact in everyday life may well be a more important way that God is embodied in the world.

When the whole community cares for each other, it reflects God's own care for the people. In similar ways, God constructs alternative communities, not honoring the time-bound customs of socially privileged families, but instead bringing together people of different genders, ages, and races to care for each other. Just as God formed a family with Hagar to raise Ishmael, the community takes in Naomi and Ruth and cares for them. In both of these nontraditional families, new life and new possibility blossom in places where pain and alienation had ruled, and in situations where racism, oppression, and disaster had stolen hope from people. When we readers see compassion that transcends custom and social division in the story of Ruth, we may catch a glimpse of the nature of God.

Spreading the Vision of God

In the early years of the Christian church, there was a great uncertainty about how to interpret the significance of Jesus. One of the early attempts to explain Jesus became a poem that may well have been a hymn sung in Christian worship not more than a decade or two after Jesus' ministry (Phil. 2:5–11). It emphasized that Jesus the Christ (or the Messiah, which represents the Hebrew word that means anointed, just as Christ means) came down to earth and accepted human form.

According to this hymn, when Jesus the Messiah was "found in human form," Jesus was humbled. That is, Jesus was not one of the power people of society. He was not born to a king or to a high priest's family. Jesus did not become human in order to be Caesar or emperor, or to lead a mass uprising and become a mighty military leader, or to become a merchant and own a wealthy estate of world renown. None of these positions of power was the place to look for God incarnate.

Although God works with people through human leaders, the positions of power become increasingly unlikely places to find God's presence and activity in the world. When Jesus became incarnate and took on human form, he chose the form of a slave, an unprivileged one. The result was death, and the reality of that death is that it was a murder, an assassination, an execution, like that accorded to any state criminal. God's work among the people takes place at the bottom of society's ordering, and it takes place at the edge of life itself, even at the most awful death.

In the incarnation of Jesus, God works within human life at life's very edges and at the margins of society, far away from the centers of power.

The search for God and God's activity in the world can easily find itself distracted by the beautiful sights of the world's power and privilege. Such a search may not be in vain; there are leaders such as Moses or Josiah who embody God's compassion for the world and who make God's care tangible for all people to know God's will and God's love. However, the more likely place to find God is along the margins of the world—where people are starving, thirsty, homeless, imprisoned, bereaved, exiled, enslaved, oppressed, forgotten, and dying. In these places are God's presence and God's ability to change the world.

Paul uses the hymn about Jesus the Messiah in Philippians 2 to make a point. Paul takes it for granted that God can be found active in the work, the life, and the death of Jesus. Paul wishes to use this sure knowledge to exhort his readers into a certain kind of lifestyle.

Therefore, my beloved, just as you have always obeyed me, not only in my presence, but much more now in my absence, work out your own salvation with fear and trembling; for it is God who is at work in you, enabling you both to will and to work for God's good pleasure.

Do all things without murmuring and arguing, so that you may be blameless and innocent, children of God without blemish in the midst of a crooked and perverse generation, in which you shine like stars in the world. (Phil. 2:12–15)

Paul's desire for his readers is not that they agree with his theological formulations, but that they take action because of their experience of God with them in the world. Paul emphasizes that God is at work in them, and therefore they must work out their own salvation; the people must seek their own ways to embody the God who is in them.

The point of incarnation, to Paul, is not that God came into the world through Jesus, or that Jesus chose human form. Instead, the point is that God always chooses common vessels for God's work, just as Jesus chose the form of a slave who was executed as a state criminal. Likewise, God chooses us as the embodiment of God's compassion in the present day. God's work is not waiting for the emperors and rich people to do it; God is present and active in common people like us to do God's will and work in this day. Paul encourages us to shine forth like stars. Perhaps Paul has in mind one of the ancient concepts of stars, that they are windows or tiny ripped holes in the sky, through which the light of heaven shines into the night. In this way of thinking, the star is not anything in and of itself, unlike how we think of stars as huge balls of flaming plasma. A star is a hole through which light shines, and we too are the embodiment of God's light when God, who is at work within us, is visible throughout the world because of what we do as those in whom God dwells.

Seeing through the Invisible

When Moses saw God, the experience of that vision changed him permanently. Certainly, when Moses saw the bush burn, it made him turn aside to see what was happening, and that brought him within shouting distance of God (Exod. 3). Moses heard God's voice, experienced God's call upon his life, and after that he embarked upon a new course of life that included a deeper service of God than Moses had ever imagined. All of that was the result of the day Moses turned from his path to investigate a burning bush, but that was not when he saw God.

Years later, when the Israelites had escaped Egypt and were in their wilderness wanderings, Moses ascended Mount Sinai and received from God the tablets of God's own instruction for the people, including the words still remembered as the Ten Commandments. In that encounter, Moses saw God. Afterward, Moses did not have the same appearance (Exod. 34:29–35). Seeing God changed Moses. It made others see in Moses a reflection of God in a shining face that scared them. Moses wore a veil in order to keep this image of God from frightening people on a day-to-day basis, but the shining allowed Moses a sense of authority when he spoke God's commandments to the people from that day forward.

Paul wrote to the early Christians in Corinth about this ancient event (2 Cor. 3:7–18). This discussion is difficult, but he ends by talking about vision.

> And all of us, with unveiled faces, seeing the glory of the Lord as reflected in a mirror, are being transformed into the same image from one degree of glory to another; for this comes from the Lord, the Spirit. (2 Cor. 3:18)

In the midst of Jesus and the spirit, we see God all the more clearly. Our vision increases. It is still not direct, clear sight. Our vision of God is not perfect. Instead, it is indirect. We see the reflection of God. Paul talks about this vision as being "reflected in a mirror." Together, we peer into a mirror, and as we see ourselves looking into that mirror, we see each other's faces and begin to see God in our sisters and brothers who join us in the search. It is a slow process as we try to discern God's image by looking at each other, who are created in God's image. It is never an exact science, and it always carries the risks of idolatry if even for a moment we mistake even the best image for the full reality of God.[2] But in each other, we see God.

As a result, as we stare into the mirrors of each other to see God, we are transformed by what we see. Our faces start to glow, and we ourselves become the image of God that others can see. We spread the vision of God into the world that has not seen God, but that can see us. As Paul told the Philippians, we are like shining stars to make God's image visible in the world's deepest night. As was written in John's first letter,

---

[2]Sallie McFague, *Models of God: Theology for an Ecological, Nuclear Age* (Philadelphia: Fortress Press, 1987), points toward the need as expressed in deconstructive theologies to move beyond our childish "nostalgia for Presence" and to develop an "ability to endure absence, uncertainty, partiality, [and] relativity" (p. 25).

Beloved, we are God's children now; what we will be has not yet been revealed. What we do know is this: when God is revealed, we will be like God, for we will see God as God is. (1 John 3:2)

When we are like God, as we come closer to appearing all the time we stare into the mirror of God and each other, we begin to see God all the more clearly. The world sees God in us, and God once more walks in the world in human form.

In the end, our love for God drives us to see God in unexpected places and eventually to realize that our beloved was nearby all along, in the form of others.

3

THE PRESENT SPIRIT

Humans relate to each other as embodied beings, but the connections between people can grow to a point that is more than physical and mechanical. We talk of it as something deeper and perhaps something spiritual. In relationships with this kind of connection, it can seem that we are reading each other's minds. We can attain the kind of closeness in which every moment is a wonder. Even predictable routines reveal something new and marvelous. When we know people this well, we can still be surprised by their thoughts, but things make sense because it all fits together. The depth of knowledge seems magical, mystical, the stuff of legends, and even spiritual. Each word uttered seems full of meaning, echoing a thousand stories of a shared past and intimating a lifetime of a future together yet to enjoy. Even the silences and the times apart are full of the relationship that unites.

Our relationship with God can take on this kind of intensity as well. God's presence is spiritual, as well as fully embodied. The relationship is experienced even in the body's absence, in the images, the memories, the words said and thought, the silences, the shared past, and the anticipated future. The biblical tradition emphasizes incarnation but also reflects that people know God at a distance. When God remains elusively absent, in days when believers do not see God's body, we may yet experience God's spiritual presence.

The Push of the Spirit

Spirits are notoriously difficult to notice, to locate, to isolate, and to define.[1] How do we know when we have seen a spirit or felt its touch? It is nearly impossible to know. In the Bible the difficulty is even greater. The Hebrew word *ruach* appears many times throughout the Old Testament, but it can mean spirit or wind or breath. Likewise, the New Testament's Greek word *pneuma* can mean a similar range of things. Every time the word occurs, a translator must make a judgment about which English word best represents the word in the Bible—and not all translators make the same decision. Even when an English translation uses the word *spirit*, the reader must beware—other possibilities may be just as legitimate, or even might be more accurate.

This interpretive problem exists from the Bible's first mention of spirit. In the beginning of the book of Genesis, God's spirit may be involved or may not be, depending upon the translation. The *New Revised Standard Version* reads this way:

> In the beginning when God created the heavens and the earth, the earth was a formless void and darkness covered the face of the deep, while a wind from God swept over the face of the waters. (Gen. 1:1–2)

But the bottom of the page in an NRSV Bible contains a note after the phrase "a wind from God," which explains that maybe the translators should have written "the spirit of God."[2] Is this the first place in the biblical story that God's spirit appears? It depends on the translation, and the language of the text leaves uncertainty.

The word *ruach* here clearly indicates a personal presence of God with strong, forceful, powerful results. God is present over the face of

---

[1]For an instructive and evocative discussion of the spirit, see Rebecca Button Prichard, *Sensing the Spirit: The Holy Spirit in Feminist Perspective* (St. Louis: Chalice Press, 1999). Cf. the comments in McFague, *Body of God,* 143–50.

[2]Also, the word usually translated as "God" may be translated as "mighty" in some cases, so the NRSV offers another possible translation for "wind of God," which is "a mighty wind." Most scholars think that this is less likely than "wind" or "spirit" in this context, and many think that "breath" is possible also.

the waters. God's presence is like the wind; it is also like a spirit. Feeling the spirit of God is much like feeling the wind; it may be strong or soft, fleeting or persistent, forceful or calming, but it is always hard to pinpoint, difficult to explain, uneasy to define. God's spirit may be hard to understand and impossible to see, but that does not mean that it is not there or that it does not have real, palpable effects. The spirit is like the wind.

God's presence is never easy to locate. One can almost never tell if the strange sensation one feels is the spirit of God, just a strong wind, or something else entirely. Yet its cumulative effects are astounding, including all creation. It is hard to sense a spirit that is virtually everywhere.[3] God's spirit pushes until its presence is made known. God's spirit is also a physical presence; God's spirit makes itself felt, even if we cannot grasp it with our fingers, let alone see it with our eyes.

Powerful and surprising things happen when God's spirit is present. Elijah was a prophet of God whose task it was to serve as God's voice to the leaders of God's people in a time when the kings refused to listen directly to God. Elijah received words from God (1 Kgs. 17:2–4, 8–9, 14, 16, 24; 18:1–2; 21:17–19, 23; 2 Kgs. 1:3–4, 16–17); he spoke words to God that God heard and obeyed (1 Kgs. 17:20–22; 18:36–38); he had conversations with God (1 Kgs. 19:9–18); he received visits from angels (1 Kgs. 19:5–8; 2 Kgs. 1:3–4, 15), as well as wild animals that may have been God's messengers too (1 Kgs. 17:6); and at the end of his life, God took Elijah away in a whirlwind that lifted him up into the sky (2 Kgs. 2:1–12).

In all of these stories, there is only one direct mention of God's spirit. Elijah was talking with his friend Obadiah, who was also a prophet and a leader of God's people, but who was living in hiding while serving the evil king Ahab (1 Kgs. 18:1–16). In this conversation, Elijah wants Obadiah to tell King Ahab that Elijah is waiting to speak with him, but Obadiah complains about how unpredictably Elijah acts:

> But now you say, "Go, tell your lord that Elijah is here." As soon as I have gone from you, the spirit of the LORD will carry you I know not where; so, when I come and tell Ahab and he cannot find you, he will kill me, although I your servant have revered the LORD from my youth. (1 Kgs. 18:11–12)

---

[3]See Prichard's comments on creation spirituality in *Sensing the Spirit*, 47–49.

Obadiah finds Elijah to be uncontrollable and dangerously unpredictable, and Obadiah believes that, as a result, his association with Elijah is bound to be lethal. He refers to this as the work of the spirit of God, which carries Elijah to places Obadiah, who himself is a fervent believer, does not know. Not even God's most faithful, persistent servants understand the operations of God's spirit.

Obadiah understands Elijah's itinerancy as the work of God's spirit in ways that make the spirit seem like the wind—powerful, potentially destructive, shifting, and almost random in its directions. Although this is the only part of Elijah's story where the NRSV uses the word *spirit*, it is not the only place where the word *ruach* occurs. In the two other places, it is translated as *wind*.

Elijah staged a massive contest between his God and the gods of the king, Ahab, and the queen, Jezebel (1 Kgs. 18:20–46). This contest took place on the top of Mount Carmel. Hundreds of prophets for Baal, the other god, set up an altar and placed on it a sacrifice for their god. They prayed fervently and worshiped Baal for hours, but there was no sign that the offering was accepted. Then Elijah set up an altar for God and placed a sacrifice on it. He poured water over the wood, soaking it, but God sent fire (perhaps lightning) to strike the wood and set it on fire, showing that the offering was accepted. All the people who were watching this contest were duly impressed, and Elijah used the event to whip the crowd into a frenzy in order to slaughter the four hundred fifty prophets of Baal.

At the end of the contest, the sacrifice, and the slaughter, God finally ended the drought that had threatened the survival of the people. The coming storm would be powerful, and everyone needed to get to safety quickly.

> Then [Elijah] said, "Go say to Ahab, 'Harness your chariot and go down before the rain stops you.'" In a little while the heavens grew black with clouds and wind; there was a heavy rain. Ahab rode off and went to Jezreel. But the hand of the LORD was on Elijah; he girded up his loins and ran in front of Ahab to the entrance of Jezreel. (1 Kgs. 18:44b–46)

When the wind of God came, it brought rain to end the deadly drought. At the same time, the hand of God empowered Elijah with superhuman strength to run ahead of Ahab's chariots all the way to safety. Was this the activity of God's spirit, or were the wind and the hand of God unrelated? Perhaps God's spirit was the force that brought the life-giving rain and the same force that allowed Elijah to run to safety.

After the drought ended, the word of Elijah's slaughtering the prophets became an issue of vengeance for Jezebel, the queen. She sought out Elijah to kill him, and so Elijah found himself once more a fugitive. He went out into the desert wilderness seeking a refuge. Angels from God brought him food that gave him strength to wander for forty days and nights until he found a mountain cave that would provide a place of safety. Along the journey, Elijah had received word from God, asking, "What are you doing here, Elijah?" (1 Kgs. 19:9). God's voice and God's words followed Elijah throughout this journey, asking for an answer that Elijah did not want to give: that God's call upon Elijah's life and Elijah's mission for God continued.

In the cave on Mount Horeb, where Elijah sought refuge from Jezebel, God came to Elijah, just as God came to Moses on the top of Mount Sinai.[4]

> [God] said, "Go out and stand on the mountain before the
> LORD, for the LORD is about to pass by." Now there was a
> great wind, so strong that it was splitting mountains and
> breaking rocks in pieces before the LORD, but the LORD was
> not in the wind; and after the wind an earthquake, but the
> LORD was not in the earthquake; and after the earthquake a
> fire, but the LORD was not in the fire; and after the fire a
> sound of sheer silence. When Elijah heard it, he wrapped his
> face in his mantle and went out and stood at the entrance of
> the cave. Then there came a voice to him that said, "What
> are you doing here, Elijah?" (1 Kgs. 19:11–13)

Here again, there is wind, the same *ruach* that is spirit. In this case, the text is clear; God is not in the wind, no matter how mighty the wind is.[5] All of the natural disasters visited upon that mountain may well be the acts of God, but God is not in them. However, God does come into Elijah's hearing, after the *ruach* passes by the mountain.

---

[4]Also, this is like the story of Jesus and God's passing by on the Mount of Transfiguration, where both Moses and Elijah were present. See chapter 2.

[5]The strength of this *ruach*, which is wind and is God's spirit, is like that in Ezekiel 37, in which God's spirit/wind blows so hard that it not only shakes the rocks but sends bones flying into the air, where they miraculously strike together and eventually form skeletons that God brings back to life. See Jon L. Berquist, *Surprises by the River: The Prophecy of Ezekiel* (St. Louis: Chalice Press, 1993), 117–29.

When God arrives again, God's word is just the same as it always has been. God asks what Elijah is doing. Elijah has a mission, and his task is elsewhere. Instead, God's word pushes Elijah even further. Life with God's spirit isn't static; the wind keeps blowing, pushing all of God's people along.

Throughout the Old Testament, the spirit of God pushes in new directions, or as in Elijah's case, pushes them back to where they had once been. This happens in many ways. Sometimes God provides skill, insight, and ability in ways that make people suited for significant tasks (Exod. 31:3; 35:31); with this kind of spirit inside, people feel compelled to create and to do wonderful things. The spirit of God often brings God's word, which provides insight into what is really going on within human situations (Num. 24:2; 1 Sam. 10:6–10; 19:20). God's spirit can spur people into effective, impassioned action that brings justice to God's people (Judg. 3:10, 6:34). At times, God's spirit comes to lead people into deeper commitments to the paths that they have known that they should take; the spirit brings courage (Judg. 11:29; 1 Sam. 16:13). Occasionally, God's spirit offers a strength that is used for violence (Judg. 14:6, 19; 15:14; 1 Sam. 11:6; 16:14–23). In some cases, the spirit of God is a troubling, unsettling force that is sure to bring changes, even when those changes are not yet known; God can work within this kind of instability (Judg. 13:25).

The spirit's actions are not knowable in advance. The spirit is never predictable. God's spirit is active in events from destruction to salvation. God's spirit is dangerous, splitting mountains and calling people to risk their lives for God. Yet often the spirit brings the word of God like the voice of a loved one carried on the wind. God's voice gives insight, hope, and courage when the one whom we love is still too far away to be seen or touched.

The Play of the Spirit

In the Old Testament's wisdom literature (especially the books of Proverbs, Job, and Ecclesiastes), a different notion of God's continuing presence develops. Within ancient Israel, some of the scribes who formed a professional class of writers, bookkeepers, and archivists also engaged in philosophical pursuits, contemplating the ethics and practices of human life, as well as the nature and essence of God. They recognized that the absence of God, not God's presence, is the dominant experience of most people.[6]

For these scribes, the experience of God in daily life meant finding God in words, especially words of wisdom. In their writings, they found a sense of God made real through words that were both insightful and faithful. In wisdom, they heard the voice of God in their lives (Prov. 2:6–11; cf. 3:19–20). By doing what wisdom directs each day, people can experience God's own presence in their lives through following God's directions for living. In this way, we can experience God's presence in every interaction with creation if we act wisely.

In Proverbs 8, wisdom comes to life in the form of a woman with extraordinary access to God.[7] Wisdom knows God, so knowing Wisdom is the same as knowing God. She invites all people with discernment to come to her and to listen to her words (Prov. 8:1–6).

Life with Wisdom brings all the words of a rich and fulfilling life with God (Prov. 8:18–21). Wisdom was God's original creation, and all other creations come to God through Wisdom.

> The LORD created me at the beginning of his work,
>> the first of his acts of long ago.
> Ages ago I was set up, at the first,
>> before the beginning of the earth.
> When there were no depths I was brought forth,
>> when there were no springs abounding with water.
> Before the mountains had been shaped,
>> before the hills, I was brought forth—
> when he had not yet made earth and fields,
>> or the world's first bits of soil.
> When he established the heavens, I was there,
>> when he drew a circle on the face of the deep,
> when he made firm the skies above,
>> when he established the fountains of the deep,

---

[6]The scribes may well have acknowledged God's presence through the temple, the historical memories and writings, prophecies, angels, or manifestations, as well as through other means, but they did not focus their attention in these directions.

[7]This woman became known in later tradition as Sophia, based on the Greek word for "wisdom." Although this poem is certainly the basis for much later speculation, it makes in itself some startling claims about God's nature and activity.

> when he assigned to the sea its limit,
>> so that the waters might not transgress his
>> command,
> when he marked out the foundations of the earth,
>> then I was beside him, like a master worker;
>> and I was daily his delight, rejoicing before him
>> always,
> rejoicing in his inhabited world
>> and delighting in the human race. (Prov. 8:22–31)

Wisdom "rejoices" in God daily (8:30), and is always "rejoicing" in the human race (v. 31).[8] Wisdom is the experience that both God and humans share. Thus, God is accessible in the immediate present, but only through wisdom, which is the practice of right speech and right actions. Wisdom teaches us the words to say to each other and to God. Wisdom is the common language that both God and faithful humans speak; Wisdom is the companion and the delight that both God and humans share.

The woman called Wisdom is an intimate image, as well as a playful one. Wisdom is not a harsh mistress; she is a delight and a cause for rejoicing. God's activity with Wisdom is something that all the people can share. God embraces Wisdom, and when we humans embrace Wisdom as well, we encounter a new and deeply personal experience of God. We do not touch God, nor do we necessarily see God, but we touch the parts of Wisdom that God has touched just a moment ago, and we feel the places where we know God has first been, as early as creation and as recently as the moment just past. This sharing with God in Wisdom is playful, just as all experiences of God's words and God's spirit are playful, unpredictable, joyful, and invigorating. In our mouths, Wisdom places the words that have come directly from God's own lips. We can almost taste God.

The Spirit Who Comes

The Old Testament usually sees God's spirit as God's continuing effective presence, beginning at creation itself and persisting into contemporary daily life. Each word of God, whether uttered at time's origin or in the most recent moment, is empowered by the breath of

---

[8]The Hebrew term here translated "rejoice" may have sexual connotations, continuing the imagery of a female who cavorts with both (male) God and (male) human, serving as a connection between them.

God's spirit. The gospels tend to present the spirit of God as something yet to arrive, a matter of future expectation.

The Spirit in the Gospel of John

Of all the gospels, John is the most clear about this anticipation of the spirit whose arrival comes after Jesus. Jesus, early in a lengthy speech that follows his announcement that one of the disciples would betray him (John 13:21), tells the disciples to expect the spirit:

> "If you love me, you will keep my commandments. And I will ask the Father, and he will give you another Advocate, to be with you forever. This is the Spirit of truth, whom the world cannot receive, because it neither sees him nor knows him. You know him, because he abides with you, and he will be in you." (John 14:15–17)

Jesus speaks of the spirit that would come after his disappearance to continue his presence with the people he loves. In typical fashion, the Johannine tradition uses the metaphor of sight and vision to explain what happens. Those who have seen, known, loved, and heard Jesus also see God. They have learned to recognize what the world cannot let itself see. God has appeared to all people, but only those who love Jesus have recognized God in the world and in the flesh. Seeing the fleshly, embodied God, these followers of Jesus have learned to see even the spirit of God and to recognize it in their lives like the wind. Whether or not they see God in the flesh, whether or not they see Jesus in the human earthly body, they will know God and love God.

The spirit of God and the words of God are tied together. God's breath empowers the pronouncement of words, and in this speech is the spirit of God. With Jesus' commandments and God's speech still ringing in their ears, their eyes will not miss the sight of God among them, even if God's presence is as hard to grasp as the wind. To be filled with Jesus' commandments, to be filled with God's words, is to have the advocacy and the comfort of God's spirit alive inside. The spirit's role is to provide the continuation of Jesus' voice. The spirit will be God's ever-present voice within the community of faith.

> "Nevertheless I tell you the truth: it is to your advantage that I go away, for if I do not go away, the Advocate will not come to you; but if I go, I will send him to you.

"I still have many things to say to you, but you cannot bear them now. When the Spirit of truth comes, he will guide you into all the truth; for he will not speak on his own, but will speak whatever he hears, and he will declare to you the things that are to come." (John 16:7, 12–13)

The words of the spirit are God's own words, just as Jesus spoke God's words. The bodily absence of Jesus does not mean that God stops speaking, but merely that the words arrive without the presence of the body. In fact, God's speech is not exhausted in Jesus (cf. John 21:25).

There is a deep relationship between Jesus and these followers. They love each other intensely, and this love will transcend death. Empowered by this love and transformed by it to love each other, the followers of Jesus continue their love with God. Because those who love Jesus have learned to recognize God's voice, they will hear how God is always speaking and their love for God will keep growing.

The Spirit in the Gospel of Luke

For Luke, the story of the spirit begins before Jesus. A priest named Zechariah was serving in the temple when an angel appeared to him and announced that he and his wife, Elizabeth, would have a son in their old age (Luke 1:5–24). This boy, who would be named John, would be a special leader.

"You will have joy and gladness, and many will rejoice at his birth, for he will be great in the sight of the Lord. He must never drink wine or strong drink; even before his birth he will be filled with the Holy Spirit. He will turn many of the people of Israel to the Lord their God. With the spirit and power of Elijah he will go before him, to turn the hearts of parents to their children, and the disobedient to the wisdom of the righteous, to make ready a people prepared for the Lord." (Luke 1:14–17)

The angel of God echoes many Old Testament themes. The child will be a Nazirite who avoids alcohol, in a long tradition of persons dedicated to God's service (Num. 6, Judg. 13). The child will have the spirit of God, like Elijah. John will speak with God's wisdom.

For Luke, Jesus is not an in-breaking of God's spirit. To the contrary, God's spirit is present and active in the Old Testament and in

Jesus' time. God's spirit is a perennial factor in human life, even though not all people see it. In fact, for Luke, it is not as important what humans see; instead, the most important thing is what God sees, and John will be powerful and favored in God's sight.

The Holy Spirit enters Mary, Jesus' mother (Luke 1:35), and Elizabeth, John's mother (Luke 1:41). Zechariah is filled with God's spirit in order to praise God for John's birth (Luke 1:67). The spirit's presence is pervasive and widespread before Jesus' birth. After Jesus enters Luke's story, the spirit is still involved in the lives of other people, such as Simeon, a temple priest (Luke 2:25–28). The spirit inaugurates Jesus' ministry in his baptism, temptation, and first sermon in Nazareth (Luke 3—4).

In that Nazareth synagogue, Jesus describes his ministry as the work of the spirit in him, quoting Isaiah 61:1–2a (Luke 4:16–21). With this quote, the reader of Luke's gospel hears Jesus speak for the first time. The ministry of Jesus is the work of the spirit.

With the spirit, there is nothing new. The spirit has always been present in the world, doing God's work, pushing people into action for God, and speaking God's word to provide direction and guidance for the paths we walk in the world. The wind of the spirit brings work and word to all.

In the last scene of the gospel of Luke, after Jesus' death, he appears to the disciples.

> Then he said to them, "These are my words that I spoke to you while I was still with you—that everything written about me in the law of Moses, the prophets, and the psalms must be fulfilled." Then he opened their minds to understand the scriptures, and he said to them, "Thus it is written, that the Messiah is to suffer and to rise from the dead on the third day, and that repentance and forgiveness of sins is to be proclaimed in his name to all nations, beginning from Jerusalem. You are witnesses of these things. And see, I am sending upon you what my Father promised; so stay here in the city until you have been clothed with power from on high." (Luke 24:44–49)

All the events of Jesus' life as Messiah, including crucifixion and resurrection, are part of this fulfillment, this embodiment of word in flesh. Yet God's work in Jesus is not the completion of God's work.

The second half of what God is doing in scripture and in the world is the proclamation of repentance and forgiveness throughout the world. This is not Jesus' work; it is work done after him, in his name. It remains God's work but now in Jesus' name, with God's lingering word persisting.

To make all of this happen, Jesus promises that God will provide power: the power of God's spirit, coming from on high like a mighty wind. The story of God's work in the world through the spirit continues, therefore, in the book of Acts, which was also written by Luke. After the resurrected Jesus ascended into the skies, the disciples waited in Jerusalem for the weeks until Pentecost.

> When the day of Pentecost had come, they were all together in one place. And suddenly from heaven there came a sound like the rush of a violent wind, and it filled the entire house where they were sitting. Divided tongues, as of fire, appeared among them, and a tongue rested on each of them. All of them were filled with the Holy Spirit and began to speak in other languages, as the Spirit gave them ability. (Acts 2:1–4)

God's spirit had been with the disciples and all of God's people throughout Jesus' ministry and before, but now they receive a new power. The spirit of God comes as wind and brings speech; it even looks like tongues. Breath feels like wind and empowers the speaking of God's words.

This powerful visible manifestation of God's spirit caused an uproar. When Peter explained what they were seeing and hearing, he referred to the prophet Joel, who quoted God's talking about pouring out God's spirit upon all people (Acts 2:17–18; cf. Joel 2:28–29). Because of Jesus' ascension, the spirit of God came with wind and speech (Acts 2:33). Peter asked his hearers to be baptized and to receive the same spirit that empowered the disciples (Acts 2:38), just as it had empowered Jesus and so many others long before. The spirit continued to spread. When Gentiles began to receive the spirit, Peter and others were amazed, but they believed that God was present in the growth of the church and the spread of the spirit (Acts 10:44–48).

By the power received from the spirit, the church continued the work of Jesus, doing God's work in the world until the words of God and Jesus were known throughout the world, beginning in Jerusalem and moving even to Rome by the end of the book of Acts. In fact, the book of Acts contains numerous sermons; speech is the primary way for spreading the good news of God throughout the world. Empowered by the spirit, the church spreads God's words. Even though the whole world has not touched God nor seen God in the flesh, even though the whole world did not have the opportunity to see God in the form of Jesus or in any other human community until the church's arrival, the spirit brings the opportunity for the whole world to hear God. God is physically present, if in no other way than in the eardrums of everyone who hears the spirit and the word of God.

The Winds of Prayer

If the spirit's presence means that God is always with us, in physical form that is sensible and audible even if it is not visible and graspable, then the spirit provides us with a means of communication with God. By the spirit, the wind moves and we feel God, whether on our skin or simply in the vibrations of our eardrums, which our minds turn to sound. Through the spirit, we hear God.

Sometimes our Christian tradition has led us to think of hearing God's voice as a breathtaking experience. The old Bible movies still live in the images in our minds, and we think of hearing God's voice as a once-in-a-lifetime experience, like Moses on Sinai. Those who hear God's voice become the leaders of their generation, specially imbued with divine power for great, world-changing tasks. In these days of tabloid news at grocery store checkout lines, we are tempted to think of hearing the voice of God as something that only strange people do. Mass murderers justify their actions through stories of hearing the voice of God or some otherworldly being. God's voice seems far away from the average person.[9]

Yet the present spirit of God means that it is possible to hear God and even to speak with God. Human relationship with God is meant to be intimate, and within that close personal connection there can be the constant daily patter of shared words, communicated experiences, and voiced tendernesses. Through the spirit and through prayer, our voices mingle with God's in the interwoven speech that is the fabric of daily relationship. Through the spirit, God's words come to

[9]See Mary Donovan Turner and Mary Lin Hudson, *Saved from Silence: Finding Women's Voice in Preaching* (St. Louis: Chalice Press, 1999).

us; through prayer, we respond. Together, there is constant communication that builds the relationship with God for which we yearn.[10]

The gospel of Matthew combined many of the sayings that the early church remembered from Jesus into one long sermon, often called the Sermon on the Mount (Matt. 5—7). In this collection, prayer is one of the central concerns. The first comment about prayer is that it is to be done in secret.

> And whenever you pray, do not be like the hypocrites; for they love to stand and pray in the synagogues and at the street corners, so that they may be seen by others. Truly I tell you, they have received their reward. But whenever you pray, go into your room and shut the door and pray to your Father who is in secret; and your Father who sees in secret will reward you. (Matt. 6:5–6)

This is not an injunction against the kinds of corporate prayer spoken out loud that occur regularly in public worship in Jewish, Christian, or Muslim traditions.[11] That kind of prayer is an opportunity for many to pray together. Instead, these words of Jesus speak against prayers that do not have the purpose of edifying the one praying or establishing any relationship with God, but have the sole purpose of impressing eavesdroppers. Prayer is not a chance to tell the whole world about how much one loves God. The time for announcing and explaining the love of God is in preaching and public worship; personal prayer has a different purpose.[12] Prayer is to be "in secret" because it is private. Jesus' direction that prayer should be secret—occurring only behind closed doors—is probably an exaggeration, as occurs often within the Sermon on the Mount. Still, the point is relevant: Prayer is meant for a purpose, which is to establish,

---

[10]For an understanding of spirit and prayer, see Prichard, *Sensing the Spirit,* 118–20.

[11]The passage asks Jesus' followers to avoid being like certain ones who pray at synagogues and at street corners. This is not a condemnation of all Jewish worship. Those who pray at street corners may not even be Jews, but may be Gentile practitioners of Greek or Roman religions. Jesus here does not speak against Jewish worship per se, but merely against certain showy forms of religious practice and against anyone praying for the wrong reasons.

[12]Note that Matthew's Sermon on the Mount includes prayer among a collection of other ethical acts. In these chapters, all of the topics focus on acts of individual piety and expression of faith. The material in the sermon is like that of ancient Old Testament wisdom traditions; public worship in Jewish or early Christian experiences never becomes the topic in these passages.

maintain, and grow a relationship with God that is intimate and powerful. Therefore, the relationship is nurtured with speech, including the speech of prayer.

Not only does Jesus encourage prayer by his followers, but he also provides a sample prayer as a model for them to pray. Through the many centuries, Christianity has called this the Lord's Prayer, and many churches recite this in worship on a regular basis in one of many translations or formats (such as that in Luke 11:2–4).

> Our Father in heaven,
>> hallowed be your name.
>> Your kingdom come.
>> Your will be done,
>>> on earth as it is in heaven.
>> Give us this day our daily bread.
>> And forgive us our debts,
>>> as we also have forgiven our debtors.
>> And do not bring us to the time of trial,
>>> but rescue us from the evil one. (Matt. 6:9b–13)

This prayer covers many of the essentials of prayer. It begins with praise, uplifting God, whose very name is special. The prayer longs for the day when God's desires will come into reality not only in heaven but also throughout the earth; thus, the prayer realizes the present reality and acknowledges that the world has plenty of disappointments mingled in with rich promise, even for God. The one who prays this makes a self-commitment to want what God wants for the world. The prayer asks for God to provide what is needed for sustenance, but not for anything unreasonable, just for enough bread for the day. Then is the recognition of the deep interconnectedness of the world as a whole; we all owe things to others, having far more debts to people than we can repay. Life with God and life with other people are matters of grace, of unpaid debts written off and forgotten. We live best when we relate to each other through our giving, not through what we owe. For much the same reason, the world contains dangers and evils from which we need to be rescued and saved. Not all dangers are avoidable, and the prayer does not expect that every bad thing can be avoided, even by God's action in the world. The prayer shares with God a longing for days when persecution and evil are gone.

Prayer, like all intimate communication, is about values and sharing. In this prayer, people and God come together in shared speech in order to speak together about what is most important and to affirm that these important things are held in common. In the depths of this spiritual relationship, we learn to want what God wants, just as God wants what is best for all of us. Prayer and spirituality are means of shaping our desires so that we want the best for ourselves, for the other, and for the world as a whole. Prayer is the longing and the yearning of the spirit given voice, spoken in soft whispers to the one whom we love and whose love for us we feel near, through the spirit.

If prayer is the whispering between intimates of the values shared between them, it is no surprise that prayer becomes so important in the early church, which lived in the aftermath of Jesus' disappearance and in the presence of God's spirit. Paul closed one of his letters with a long admonition about how the believers should live together.

> But we appeal to you, brothers and sisters, to respect those who labor among you, and have charge of you in the Lord and admonish you; esteem them very highly in love because of their work. Be at peace among yourselves. And we urge you, beloved, to admonish the idlers, encourage the fainthearted, help the weak, be patient with all of them. See that none of you repays evil for evil, but always seek to do good to one another and to all. Rejoice always, pray without ceasing, give thanks in all circumstances; for this is the will of God in Christ Jesus for you. Do not quench the Spirit. Do not despise the words of the prophets, but test everything; hold fast to what is good; abstain from every form of evil. (1 Thess. 5:12–22)

In this passage the central comment to "pray without ceasing" gives a clue to the life of prayer and spirit that runs throughout this passage. Prayer is not the recitation of words designed to move God into action or some religious formula to be repeated to prove one's piety, enhance one's moral fiber, or create a sense of comfort or inner peace. Prayer is the love between intimates, in the form of shared values and whispers of commitment and emotion. There is always time for whispers like this. The spirit is alive and never quenched when this kind of prayer becomes central to the community and to the lives of its members.

Prayer, like the spirit, does not make life easy. To the contrary, life with the spirit and life connected to God in prayer can be quite unsettling. The spirit is invasive and intrusive. Elijah was moved by the spirit—that is, Elijah was pushed and prodded to new places and to unwanted activities by the spirit. The spirit is God's wisdom, which may push people to courses of action that they would not have chosen themselves. Yet the spirit is notoriously difficult to avoid. The spirit is as pervasive as the wisdom with which God created the world; it is impossible to live life without the spirit, even though it is amazingly easy to live in ignorance of it. Like the wind, we cannot block the spirit from our lives.

The Touch of the Wind

God's spirit formed us at creation and guides us through life. God works in the world through spirit and through wind, and so it is not at all surprising that God works in human lives in the same way. This presence is constant and palpable, even when God cannot be touched or seen.

> Likewise, the Spirit helps us in our weakness; for we do not know how to pray as we ought, but that very Spirit intercedes with sighs too deep for words. And God, who searches the heart, knows what is the mind of the Spirit, because the Spirit intercedes for the saints according to the will of God. (Rom. 8:26–27)

The spirit's invasive presence knows us inside, just as God searches our hearts (Ps. 51). The result is speech, carried upon the spirit's breath, that binds us ever closer to God.

When God walked among humans in visible form, God could be seen, touched, and grasped. God's tangible incarnation meant a certainty to God. Talking with God involved gestures, touches, eye contact, and all those other elements of communication that make it a complete and fulfilling event. When God can be seen, even in reflections of others, there is a certain confidence in God's appearance. But when God is known in spirit, the experience has a more tenuous sensation. As spirit and as wind, God is closer than life itself; we breathe God into our very beings with each moment's breath. But the spirit cannot be seen or touched. It carries speech, but sometimes its words are barely audible. Uncertain as to whether we heard the spirit of God or not, we are left asking each other, "Did you hear that?" If we could see God, touch God, or read God's lips, we would know with so much more certainty what God's presence in our lives was about.

The spirit is so close to us, yet too close to see. It is like a ghost, just a trace of God's presence, still real, yet almost beyond belief and certainly beyond certainty. Like wind, we may see where God's spirit has been, but we never see the spirit itself. Even when we observe the leaves' rustle or hear a high whistle, we are never quite sure what we see and hear. Is it the wind? Is it God's spirit? What we feel inside, what we experience within our souls, can be so hard to reconcile with the sights that everyone can see. God's present closeness and inner dwelling are so evasive.

Our own desire is deeply intertwined with our experience of the spirit. In a sense the spirit is a trace in the sand, an afterimage on the retina, a memory, a longing, a desire. Because of the intensity and intimacy of our relationship with God, we miss God when God is out of range of our own senses' grasp and sight. So we hear things, and we feel an insubstantial brush on our skins in the same way we hear and feel wind, breath, and spirit. Some may ask if we made this up out of the stuff of our own longings, and perhaps the question cannot be answered by those who do not feel God's breath. The experience is internal, and the idea that what has made a difference is the spirit's touch is more a hunch than anything of certainty at all—just as when we observe a breeze, which is hardly anything substantial but is quite real and powerful nonetheless. To feel desire, longing, love, or passion is much like feeling the wind or feeling the spirit. It is elusive and hardly ever certain, and it often leaves us wanting more.

4

THE DANGER OF GOD WITH US

There may be nothing more miraculous than the wind, nothing that more fully expresses and embodies the wonder of life—the feel of the wind on one's face, a cool breeze on a summer evening, the wind's roar and the waves' crash along the coast, the gentlest tufts of air tossing snowflakes in magical spirals, the grace of sailboats on bright sunny days, the wind that makes people cuddle together for warmth, the wind that keeps aloft the high-flying birds, the race of puffy clouds across crystal blue heavens, the intricate curves of the tree growing gnarled in the wind's face, the soft susurrations of tenderness caressing a lover's hair. Moments like these testify to God's nature and presence, a grace and gift beyond words.

There may be nothing more terrible and terrifying than the wind—the gales that bring harsh storms, the hideous look of destructive storms glowering on a horizon and crouching before they pounce, hail pummeling from side to side, windshears that bring down planes, windstorms that toss over buses, winds that bring sand to cover crops and bury them in death's embrace, winds that rip bricks off buildings and turn timber into chaff blown helter-skelter across the landscape, hot winds pushing fire's consumption through forest and field, wind-driven lightning that crackles and strikes and scorches, dust devils, whirlwinds, waterspouts, cyclones, hurricanes, tornados. These speak only of terror beyond words.

God is with us like the wind. The Old and New Testaments both describe God as spirit, breath, and wind in our midst, always present, palpable upon our skin yet never graspable, and visible only in the effects upon other objects. When the Bible ventures into these images and metaphors for God, the texts begin to speak of the unpredictability of God. God can be like the winds of terror, as well as the winds of grace. God, like the wind, is not contained, nor even easily categorized.[1]

The danger of life with God is not merely an unintended and somewhat unfortunate side effect of the Bible's metaphors. These images are no accident, for the biblical idea of God's presence carries within it a deep ambiguity. God is present, physically present within our world. But there is a sense in which we may not want God so near. The concept of God may not be so scary, but the reality of God can indeed be frightening. It can be wonderful to have God with us, but God has a mind of God's own. Living together is always hard, all the more so when the other is strong willed, and perhaps never more than when the one with whom we live is God.

God, like wind, is uncontrollable. Although we believe that God works in our best interest, we do not really understand what our own best interest is, and so God's actions at times appear to work against us. At least, that is the traditional Christian way of understanding why God's presence in our lives can feel negative at times. Other lines of thinking have emphasized God's absence and withdrawal or God's limits and inability to do what we want. But the biblical traditions offer a different perspective: God is not controllable and not even understandable. When humans live together, they think they know each other, but there is always surprise, even after years. Some people question if the relationship is such a good thing after all. The love and

---

[1]Theology has recognized that God cannot be contained in human language and that we must speak of God in metaphors that are evocative but ever inexact. At the same time, theology has understood that God is destabilizing, yet contemporary theology has not progressed as far as our most ancient scriptural traditions in realizing how incomprehensible God is.

the trust may be enough to survive such times, but the questions arise nonetheless. In life with God, who is so much more different from us than a human partner could ever be, we experience times when God seems totally beyond our comprehension, when God seems out of control and dangerous. We cannot ignore those times because we live too close to God to just close our eyes and forget. If we could explain those times away, that would mean that we could fit God into our own categories of thought. God cannot be psychoanalyzed; God's actions cannot be explained away, even by the most intricate of speculative philosophical theologies. Many of these theologies try to defend God by claiming that some of the Bible's images are reliable and normative, but others must be discarded or judged as less true. However, a biblical theology must be willing to explore the Bible's images without prejudging which are more central or authoritative than others. The biblical notion of God is of one who lives very close to us, who is intimately involved with humanity, but who remains fundamentally other than us, not understandable and certainly not reducible to our theological systems or to our own wishes of what God should be like. God remains the stranger in our midst, no matter how long we have lived together and how close we have become.

There is a danger to living with God. To be honest, living with any being is dangerous, whether human, animal, or divine. Togetherness and closeness mean risk; it means dealing with the other in intimate ways. There are frustrations, mysteries, puzzles, consternations, accidents, hurts, and pains—in addition to the joys of life together. If God is the perfect partner and acts always in ways that lead to the harmonies of domestic bliss, the rest of us are not so good at relationships. We hurt ourselves through our own expectations and accidents, even if God is not to blame for any of them. We humans do not experience life together without both pain and joy. Life with a God who is physically present means that there are dangers, risks, and times of terror. There may well be moments when we want our privacy, when we wish God would give us a little space, when we just want to be alone, or when we wish God would go far away. Relationships are rocky, always difficult even when they seem easy, constantly shifting, ever tenuous. As partner, God is no different. If we believe that we and God share the same image and likeness, maybe God experiences these things too.

We Never Capture the Wind

In relationships we never fully know each other. Knowledge is a difficult thing; it is always slippery even in the best of circumstances. None of us really know ourselves, no matter how much time we spend in introspection, self-help, or therapy. Much less do we know each other. People remain mysterious, unexplainable, unknown, and unknowable. Even if we have known someone all our lives, we can still be surprised. Each person in the world is unique, nonreplaceable, and special. Like two snowflakes or two fingerprints, no two look alike, think alike, or act alike. Certainly, there are similarities, and it is easy to draw generalities, but in the specifics of daily life those generalities fail to help.

The other seems beyond comprehension. We may get used to the patterns, but this does not mean that we understand them. The human relationship with God partakes of the same reality and has to live within the same limits. We do not understand God. In fact, the situation with God is much more severe because God's thoughts and actions are not very much like ours. The prophet Isaiah reflected on this.

Seek the LORD while God may be found,
    call upon God while God is near;
let the wicked forsake their way,
    and the unrighteous their thoughts;
let them return to the LORD, that God may have mercy
    upon them,
    and to our God, who will abundantly pardon.
For my thoughts are not your thoughts,
    nor are your ways my ways, says the LORD.
For as the heavens are higher than the earth,
    so are my ways higher than your ways
    and my thoughts than your thoughts.
    (Isa. 55:6–9)

God does not think like we do, and so God does not act like we do. Basic, fundamental differences are at the very core of our relationship with God. The love that binds us into life together is fraught with irreconcilable differences. All of God's actions remain unknowable, unexplainable, incomprehensible, unpredictable. Living with God is like living with the wind, and we never can guess which way the wind will blow.

But we long to know God, so we are tempted to reduce God to something we can understand. This may be the chief impulse behind idolatry. One of the earliest stories of idol worship within the Bible occurred when God's people had followed Moses into the wilderness, out of Egyptian slavery. They faced the uncertainties of that wild desert. Even though they had a pillar of fire and of cloud to follow each day, they never knew where God's spirit would blow. They did not see God, they did not hear God's voice, they could not touch God, and they could not predict God's directions in that pillar. Then Moses disappeared; he went up the mountain to talk with God and find out what was going on, but day after day he did not return. Without any communication, they felt cut off from God.

> When the people saw that Moses delayed to come down from the mountain, the people gathered around Aaron, and said to him, "Come, make gods for us, who shall go before us; as for this Moses, the man who brought us up out of the land of Egypt, we do not know what has become of him."
>
> Aaron said to them, "Take off the gold rings that are on the ears of your wives, your sons, and your daughters, and bring them to me."
>
> So all the people took off the gold rings from their ears, and brought them to Aaron. He took the gold from them, formed it in a mold, and cast an image of a calf; and they said, "These are your gods, O Israel, who brought you up out of the land of Egypt!" (Exod. 32:1–4)

Because the people did not know what had happened to Moses, they wanted a god that they could see, so they had Aaron make for them a golden calf to worship. They replaced God, whom they did not see or understand, with an inanimate object that was completely comprehensible and utterly predictable. After all, the calf was made with gold from the rings in their own ears, and so it was perfectly simple to understand where it came from. Because it was an object, it was not going to move; it would give them no surprises at all. They had reduced God to an image of their own making.

Idolatries of all sorts work the same way. We replace God with what we can understand, see, touch, and grasp. We choose inanimate objects over the live relationship with a partner who is very difficult to comprehend and impossible to predict. Although we rarely make golden calves these days, we have no end of other idolatries. If we know what it takes to get ahead in the world, we choose what we know instead of the frustrating mystery of who God is and what God is trying to do in the world. Taking care of ourselves and those whom we love becomes the ultimate value instead of life lived with a God whose interests may not coincide with what we want for ourselves. Money, career, security, comfort, and a host of other values become the gods whom we worship. Around these idols arise priesthoods and hierarchies of those who tell us that they know the best way to gain advantage in the world. Whether they are kings or presidents, economists or analysts, theologians or ministers, they claim to know God, but they are peddling a reduced version of the truth. Instead of worshiping a God whose ways are beyond ours, they want us to follow them in service to false gods of understandable security and diminished vision. The leaders who claim they know God are among the most dangerous pitfalls we face in our attempt to know and love an unknowable God.

More subtle idolatries in the church occur any time that we begin to understand God or to deceive ourselves into thinking that we do. We create intellectual systems that strive to touch God. In complicated philosophical propositions and arguments, we begin to think that we understand God. In creeds and statements of God's promises, we begin to believe that we can predict God. We tell ourselves that these few sentences, or even the almost infinite complexity of the Bible's many pages, encapsulate the essential truth of God. But God is never reduced to words, especially not the words of human theories about God. The personal reality of an intimate yet unknowable God is never the same as a set of sentences, no matter how much truth and insight is in those words. God is beyond any theology.

All idolatry reduces the gulf between God and humanity. The huge distance between our own understanding and the nature of God frightens us, but it is the difference that powers the relationship. Of course, Isaiah knows that this vast difference is not a reason to avoid true relationship with God. The prophet never suggests that we should stop loving God or living with God because of the differences between us.[2] Again, there are parallels with human relationships.

---

[2]Other biblical traditions are clearer than Isaiah that life without God is not really possible.

Relationships are built on a foundation of the many slippery, shifting differences between partners. We never entirely know the other, and there certainly cannot be agreements on every part of daily life. Relationships are about the accommodation of difference more than they are about anything else. The individualities that each partner brings to the relationship are what make it rich and fulfilling, whether the relationship is marriage, partnership, love, friendship, companionship, business, or any of a thousand other possible configurations. Difference drives relationship; variety is, as they say, the spice of life. Yet none of these human relationships face the degree of differences that exists between us and God. The distance between us and the God we cannot understand is a huge gulf.

The Power of God

In part, it would be right to point to the difference in power as the key difference. In human relationships, there are always differences in power. In work relationships where hierarchies of authority structure the business environment, such differences are perpetually clear, and even in the companies that try to be less hierarchical, reminders are everywhere of the power differences, from the corner offices with windows on upper floors to the size of the desks, from the way that people dress to the way that they talk, from the matters of who runs meetings to who sets the rules for others. In our culture, we become used to the power differences in the workplace, and perhaps we even get so accustomed to them that they no longer seem problems—they are simply the way things are, and we forget that power differences can be evil ways of negating the worth of some people for the benefit of others.

Relationships at home can partake of the same inequalities. Despite how much we think that the second half of the twentieth century has brought the Western world new possibilities of equality and has ushered in a new level of democracy and basic human rights worldwide, the patterns of power are replicated in almost every home. The culture drives these inequalities through the expectations in media almost as well as through the large-scale underpayment of women and of racial and ethnic minorities. Within many households, the gender gap still exists; the power differences between men and women can be as subtle as the sexism that pervades the whole society or as blatant as statements about the differences between women and men or between men's roles and women's roles, and at times the power differences are enforced with angry words, debilitating withdrawal, and even the physical terrors of punches, kicks, and rapes. Within the world as we know it, no relationships completely escape the differences of power that drive our culture in its frenzied climb.

What does this mean about our relationship with God? Is this relationship also one of power differences? Should we think of that power difference as benign, as simply the way things are, or as a source of danger in our lives? Life with God always carries the danger that is inevitable when we live with someone so much more powerful than we are, especially when the powerful one is incomprehensible and unpredictable. With a breath of wind and spirit, God can heal, save, and sustain. God can also destroy. God has been known to do both.

Isaiah reminds us that God is extremely accessible (Isa. 55:6–9). God is to be sought and God can be found. God is not some distant being who inhabits only far-off heavens. God can be found. We can call on God, and God will hear us. More than that, God will have mercy on us and pardon us. Even though those very concepts echo the power and danger inherent in this relationship, the words also carry the promise that God's love will win out over the danger. God is faithful, and the gulfs of knowledge and power still leave a possibility for relationship.

Still, it is difficult and always frustrating to love what we do not understand. It is hard enough to live in relationship with those who make sense to us most of the time. With God, it will never be that easy. There is even a danger in a close relationship with the unknowable, a danger of the loss of something essential in the self. God is so strong-willed that we may lose our sense of who we are. Our individuality is at risk in such an uneven relationship, even more than it is in any other relationship. The closeness has its price. We want God's approval and favor; in Isaiah's words, we need God's mercy and pardon. What will seeking this do to us? How much of our selves will we have to give up? Our tradition has always insisted that God will not ask us to give up the good parts of ourselves because God is the one who created us and who always has our best interests at heart. But with an unknowable and unpredictable God, there will be many times when we do not see the evidence of such things, when we have no grounds to discern God's motives.

In the end, we do know God well enough to establish a relationship, but we will always face limits in that relationship. It will never be a relationship based on knowledge and understanding. Instead, it must be a relationship grounded in passion, in care, in the heat of emotion, not the cool of reason. Reason will never be strong enough to bridge the gulf in knowability that exists between us and God, but love may well prove sufficient. We must seek God with the passion and energy that love provides. Of course, understanding is not the basis for connection in human relationships anyway. We do not love God because we have come to an understanding of God that is perfect, or good, or even sufficient. We have met, we have started to get to know each other, and then we find ourselves falling in love. It is the love, not the knowledge, that binds us to God. Like those blown by the wind, we are moved by our experience with God; our hearts move within us. To love God is to feel the strange movements of this passion within us; to love God is to seek to be in relationship with one whom we cannot really understand. To fall in love with God is to throw caution to the wind.

The church's teachings have emphasized that God discloses God's self to us, through the Bible as well as through Jesus and other means, but the Bible itself insists that we will never understand. We will not fully know God. Not even God's most abundant self-disclosure can overcome the limits in our own knowledge. God's revelation is a prerequisite for relationship with God, but revelation cannot be the foundation. Meeting and getting to know each other are the first steps in a relationship of enduring love. But knowledge is not the foundation; more knowledge helps build life together, but it takes much more than knowledge. Love takes its own course, and often knowledge follows, although it is always imperfect knowledge. In the case of God, we meet, we start to get to know each other, we fall in love, and then we keep learning about what and who God is, even though everything we know is partial and partly wrong and somehow never adds up to a complete picture of our God, who is far beyond the limits of our own thoughts.

One of the other problems in loving God is that God has a surprising capacity to change. Again, the traditional theologies of the church have painted a portrait of a God who is unchanging and who is the same from the past to the present to the future. It may well be true that God is much more consistent than humans manage to be, but that does not mean that God cannot change. The Bible does not portray God as unchangeable. Instead, the Bible clearly insists that, at least sometimes, God sets forth and then undergoes a change of heart. One example of this is God's frustration with the people whom God had led out of slavery in Egypt. While the people were in the desert wilderness after their escape from Egypt, they began to complain. The terrain was miserable; the food was boring; the prospects for the future were not pleasant; they began to get on each other's nerves as traveling companions; the trip through the desert was dragging on so long that it seemed it might take forever, or at least a lifetime. Moses and God both became highly frustrated with the people's complaints.

> The LORD said to Moses, "I have seen this people, how stiff-necked they are. Now let me alone, so that my wrath may burn hot against them and I may consume them; and of you I will make a great nation."

> But Moses implored the LORD his God, and said, "O LORD, why does your wrath burn hot against your people, whom you brought out of the land of Egypt with great power and with a mighty hand? Why should the Egyptians say, 'It was with evil intent that he brought them out to kill them in the mountains, and to consume them from the face of the earth'? Turn from your fierce wrath; change your mind and do not bring disaster on your people. Remember Abraham, Isaac, and Israel, your servants, how you swore to them by your own self, saying to them, 'I will multiply your descendants like the stars of heaven, and all this land that I have promised I will give to your descendants, and they shall inherit it forever.'"

> And the LORD changed his mind about the disaster that he planned to bring on his people. (Exod. 32:9–14)

In this story, God changes God's own mind about what to do. God makes plans and announces them, and then repents and changes courses. This changeability makes relationship difficult. How can we live with God from one minute to the next when God's mind can change? What sense does it make to believe in God's promises when

God could think up something else to do, or when God's friends can talk God into doing something different?[3] There is an unpredictability in God, and God can never be controlled by human action. This means that there is almost an unreliability about God. God may be trustworthy, but we can never afford to take the next step and think that God will do what we think God will do. We cannot count on God in that way.

But the story of Moses affects our ideas of relationship with God in another way as well. God had worked hard to bring the people out of Egypt and away from the slavery that they had experienced there. Tradition rightly lists this as one of the stories that shows God as most saving. Clearly in the story, God had a massive investment in the welfare of the people. This was something God intended to do, and God had staked a huge amount of reputation on the success of this venture. Yet, in a moment of frustration, God is ready to end the whole thing. God has loved the people and has lifted them up to save them; God now seriously considers letting wrath carry God away, so that God would destroy and consume them. The saving God is ready to kill the very ones whom God has so loved. The Israelites should be grateful to Moses, for their salvation and survival depended on the wisdom and moral character of the friend in whom God confided. In the end, God did not do what God had planned. God had a change of heart. The NRSV calls God's plan a "disaster," but it is the same word that everywhere else is translated as "evil." God had evil plans, but Moses changed God's mind.

This is frightening. We want to believe in a God who is always good, but the Bible itself tells stories that point out how not even God is always good, or at least not always thinking clearly, and is ready to be swept away by the heat of anger in a moment of squabble with the people whom God loved. God takes a time-out to talk it over with a friend, and fortunately for all, Moses can talk God out of this awful thing that God had seriously contemplated. But the danger

---

[3]Church tradition has often focused on the unchanging promises of God. However, the Bible asserts that God is not bound by what God has said in the past. God's promises represent strong concerns and enduring desires. But humans do not control God; God remains persistently beyond human grasp. If God promises to do something, we have no way of holding God responsible for it. If God promises to react to our actions in some particular way, we cannot afford to think that our own action will force God to do something—even if God promised it would. Promises and statements of intention do not mean that God is required to do what we want. We must not reduce our love with God to a cause-and-effect matter with ourselves as the cause.

is there, and it does not go away. As in any relationship, our love affair with God has moments of frustration and disappointment. In those moments, things can go wrong—sometimes things can go horribly, abusively, murderously wrong. It is bad enough that God is not consistent, is not unchangeable, is not predictable; but God can think and act in anger the dimensions of which are beyond human understanding, for God's ways and thoughts are far beyond ours.

The Dangers of Relationship

Our life with this incarnate, embodied God is a relationship of closeness, intimacy, and depth, and when the Bible speaks of this relationship, it often discusses the situation in terms of other intimate human relationships, especially the relationship of marriage between a man and a woman. In these cases, the man in the metaphor usually represents God, and the woman usually represents the people whom God loves and with whom God wishes to live. Their relationship is intimate, sexual, and powerful.

In ancient Israel, the institution of marriage was very different from contemporary notions of marriage. Often, the man purchased the woman who would join his household, in many cases from her father. Marriages were not often the result of love between two people; instead, marriages were frequently formed for economic, social, and sometimes political reasons. The chief man of the household owned and controlled those within the household. Although some households were much more egalitarian than others, the culture as a whole reinforced a strong patriarchy in which elder men dominated others. This relationship serves as a metaphor for how God relates to people. God is the chief of the household and possesses a power to enforce God's will that others in the household do not have. Others must answer to God, whether God's requests and demands are right or not, but God is responsible to no one.

The prophet Jeremiah sees God in terms like this. God is the powerful one who overpowers God's partners in relationship. When God makes Jeremiah speak, Jeremiah must do just as God says, no matter what negative repercussions result.

> O LORD, you have enticed me,
> and I was enticed;
> You have overpowered me,
> and you have prevailed.

I have become a laughingstock all day long;
>   Everyone mocks me.
For whenever I speak, I must cry out,
>   I must shout, "Violence and destruction!"
For the word of the LORD has become for me
>   a reproach and a derision all day long.
If I say, "I will not mention him,
>   or speak any more in his name,"
Then within me there is something
>   like a burning fire shut up in my bones;
I am weary with holding it in,
>   And I cannot. (Jer. 20:7–9)

In Jeremiah's view, God is one who has pushed an alien will upon him. God controls Jeremiah's words and actions, and this control has been most detrimental to Jeremiah. God does not have Jeremiah's best interest at heart; God's demands mean that Jeremiah faces danger every day in every place that the prophet goes. It is impossible for Jeremiah to prevent himself from doing what God wants to do because God has overpowered Jeremiah.

The opening verses of this passage are capable of supporting many different translations, but all of them are serious condemnations of God's actions in regard to Jeremiah. In the NRSV, God has "enticed" Jeremiah, which led to the overpowering and to the diminishment of Jeremiah's own ability and will. The first verb could also be translated as seduction: "You have seduced me, and I was seduced." But even that is not quite right because seduction is not quite strong enough. The clear intent here is that God deceived Jeremiah. God is not just making an offer that Jeremiah finds attractive, even irresistably attractive. God makes Jeremiah an offer that is not what it seems; God is not being honest with Jeremiah. When Jeremiah begins to see through the deception and to realize what God is doing, it is too late, and God overpowers Jeremiah, operating out of God's power and not out of respect for Jeremiah's desires. The scene is like a date rape that begins with partial consent based on false premises and ends with brute force after the deception is uncovered. God's promises may have been attractive, but soon coercion is the only thing that characterizes the relationship between Jeremiah and God. The prophet laments that he is too tired to deal with this, that his will has been diminished in the confrontation with God's power. He has lost his ability to resist the overpowering strength that God uses to coerce Jeremiah. Jeremiah is forced to do what he does not want to do, and it is a matter of shame for him (Jer. 20:8). A few verses later, Jeremiah wishes he had never been born (Jer. 20:14–18). He would rather be dead; he would rather never have lived than face days as God's victim, no matter how wonderful their relationship had been in earlier years.

This is not the only case of God's acting this way within a prophet's vision. Ezekiel tells a story in which two sisters, Oholah and Oholibah, represent two groups of God's people in Israel and Judah. God marries the two sisters, but they seek other lovers. God's actions against them are just as terrible.

> For thus says the Lord GOD: Bring up an assembly against them, and make them an object of terror and of plunder. The assembly shall stone them and with their swords they shall cut them down; they shall kill their sons and their daughters, and burn up their houses. Thus will I put an end to lewdness in the land, so that all women may take warning and not commit lewdness as you have done. They shall repay you for your lewdness, and you shall bear the penalty for your sinful idolatry; and you shall know that I am the Lord GOD. (Ezek. 23:46–49)

Knowing God as Lord and realizing who God is are important themes for Ezekiel.[4] They echo throughout the book, and Ezekiel is not the only prophet who is constantly concerned with the proper recognition of God. But it is not easy for Ezekiel, Jeremiah, or any of the prophets to offer comforting images of God's presence and life with God. In fact, these images can be terrifying. We can tell ourselves that the point of the stories and visions is to reassure us that God loves us and really wants to have close relationships with us, while reminding us that these kinds of relationships require loyalty and commitment as well as offer amazing care and provision. God's love and care for us is like the most intense of human relationships. In that intensity is danger; God the lover can become God the spurned and jealous lover. God's anger is a fearsome thing to behold, and in

---

[4]For more on these images in Ezekiel 16 and 23 within the context of the book of Ezekiel, see Jon L. Berquist, *Surprises by the River: The Prophecy of Ezekiel* (St. Louis: Chalice Press, 1993), 41–53, 67–77; and Renita J. Weems, *Battered Love: Marriage, Sex, and Violence in the Hebrew Prophets,* Overtures to Biblical Theology (Minneapolis: Fortress Press, 1995), 58–67.

these images God directs wrath upon the ones whom God loves. These ideas about God are disturbing; God wants intimacy and yet threatens disaster just when we are most vulnerable. The power is clear, and no matter how much we tell ourselves that these are only images, the stories may haunt us with their images of abuse, rape, torture, and death.

The most intense loves can transform our whole lives, but they still leave us as individuals in our own right. We still need moments apart; we need our privacy. Yet here again the remarkable difference between us and God makes this relationship difficult. God is so much bigger and stronger than we are, and so time alone becomes nearly impossible. The relationship with us humans means so much to God, and at times we just cannot get away.

Within the Bible, there are times when people want some distance from God. Despite the religious drive for closeness to God, at times God becomes stifling. We cannot take time off from this relationship, not even a few moments to collect our thoughts or just be ourselves for a bit. When God is angry, there is no place where we can go for a little while to let things cool down between us. There is no place to hide, even when we want to be alone.

The prophet Amos offers one of the most horrifying images of wanting to get away from God. In this vision, God swears to destroy a whole people. God's goal is genocide, no matter how long it takes. Not a single household will be spared, not even a hovel that housed a family so poor that they slept ten to a room. The people cower in fear of God.

> The Lord GOD has sworn by himself (says the LORD, the God of hosts): I abhor the pride of Jacob and hate his strongholds; and I will deliver up the city and all that is in it. If ten people remain in one house, they shall die. And if a relative, one who burns the dead, shall take up the body to bring it out of the house, and shall say to someone in the innermost parts of the house, "Is anyone else with you?" the answer will come, "No." Then the relative shall say, "Hush! We must not mention the name of the LORD." (Amos 6:8–10)

Others come to this destroyed city to burn the corpses. Instead, they find a survivor, but they deny that they have found anyone; they fear that God will not stop the destruction if God finds out that there are more left. The few who are left are afraid to speak or to move or to venture out into daylight because they do not want this wrathful, vengeful God to find them. They even refuse to speak the name of God in a whisper while hiding underground in the rubble and speaking to a close relative. They want nothing to do with God, and they fear that God will hear the name and find them. When we desire time away, God does not stop. There is no refuge from God. If this relationship becomes dangerous or damaging, we have lost everything.

A relationship with God is not easy nor always comfortable. In fact, our own assurance and comfort is hardly the point. When passion drives both God and us toward each other, the relationship can be a thing of utmost beauty and joy, like the best of human loves and even more. But closeness means risk, and danger always lurks.

Loving the Wind

In our life with God it is easy to think that our closeness to God and the depth of our love for God entitle us to some sort of special treatment. With no small dose of irony, Amos reminds us that we do have something special because we are intimate with God, but it is not necessarily that for which we have hoped.

> Hear this word that the LORD has spoken against you,
>> O people of Israel, against the whole family that I
>> brought up out of the land of Egypt:
> You only have I known of all the families of the earth;
>> therefore I will punish you for all your iniquities.
> Do two walk together unless they have made an
>> appointment?
> Does a lion roar in the forest, when it has no prey?
>> Does a young lion cry out from its den, if it has
>> caught nothing? (Amos 3:1–4)

We have made an appointment with God; we have made a date; we have formed a family. But in the forest, we are ambushed. God is close to us and loves us, but God will punish God's own family more strictly than any other part of the human family. We love a God who expects much of us and who is unspeakably harsh, and because we cannot understand God, we can never quite know why these things happen, and we cannot predict how God will react. This relationship is full of the dangers that come from life with someone we do not understand and who proves dangerous for all of those who are close.

This God who loves us and who lives so near us will stay with us. There is no escape from this God. Wherever we go, God is there first. We may not understand God, but God seems to know a lot about us. One of the psalms depicts God almost like a stalker who has been watching our every move and who has information about us no one should be able to have. God hems us in, and there is no place to go to get away from God. We may experience God's searching for us as mercy or as something to frighten us; it is difficult to know which of those to feel because God is so unpredictable. We cannot get away from this one whom we cannot understand.

> O LORD, you have searched me and known me.
> You know when I sit down and when I rise up; you
>   discern my thoughts from far away.
> You search out my path and my lying down, and are
>   acquainted with all my ways.
> Even before a word is on my tongue, O LORD, you
>   know it completely.
> You hem me in, behind and before, and lay your hand
>   upon me.
> Such knowledge is too wonderful for me; it is so high
>   that I cannot attain it.
> Where can I go from your spirit? Or where can I flee
>   from your presence?
> If I ascend to heaven, you are there; if I make my bed
>   in Sheol, you are there.
> If I take the wings of the morning and settle at the
>   farthest limits of the sea,
> even there your hand shall lead me, and your right
>   hand shall hold me fast.
> If I say, "Surely the darkness shall cover me, and the
>   light around me become night,"
> even the darkness is not dark to you; the night is as
>   bright as the day, for darkness is as light to you.
>   (Ps. 139:1–12)

In the most intimate times of closeness with God, we treasure how hard God works to stay near us. This psalm can be a comforting affirmation of God's abiding, persistent, supportive presence. But there are nights when we wonder if we want God always this close, especially when we know that God has punished God's family before.

There is joy and terror in living this close to God. We love this God in the same way that one loves the wind. Then we know that God is truly other and is thus truly capable of loving us—and what a love it is.[5] But there are days of gentle breezes and days of destructive gales; we cannot predict, we cannot choose. We love the wind and live with whatever it brings, for there is no other way. Another of Israel's prophets referred to those who had lived with God when he said, "For they sow the wind, and they shall reap the whirlwind" (Hos. 8:7). What we do comes back to us. When we love God, we experience life with God, even on the days when this love feels like a threatening, terrifying whirlwind all around us. Like the whirlwind, God is unknowable, unpredictable, and unstoppable.

But on the days when the breeze lightly touches our hair or runs across our skin like a tender caress, cooling and calming and making the whole world right, who can resist loving the wind?[6]

---

[5] See Jessica Benjamin, *Like Subjects, Love Objects: Essays in Recognition and Sexual Difference* (New Haven, Conn.: Yale University Press, 1995).

[6] Cf. Mark C. Taylor, *Erring: A Postmodern A/Theology* (Chicago: University of Chicago Press, 1984), 168: "Radical christology is thoroughly incarnational. The carnality embodied in the free play of carnival and comedy overturns every form of repressive transcendence... Through unexpected twists and unanticipated turns, erring and aberrance show the death of God, disappearance of self, and end of history to be the realization of *mazing grace.*"

5

THE BIRTH OF JESUS

For many Christians, incarnation is an idea more prevalent at Christmas than at any other time of the year. The incarnation of God in Jesus, an event that happened once in history, is the way that the tradition has most often retold the story that appears four different ways in the New Testament gospels.

The usual telling of the Christmas story concentrates on how God had been absent but for the first time ever took on human flesh. This understanding of incarnation is that God never had a body, but was a spirit in heaven, until God entered human history and was born into the body of Jesus. Many theological interpretations of Jesus assert that God had never been physically present but now assumes a body for the first time. The miracle of the incarnation is that God, once distant, came close in Jesus.[1] But the clear witness of scripture is

---

[1]For introductions to the theological treatment of the concept of incarnation, see Anne Bathurst Gilson, "Incarnation," in Letty M. Russell and J. Shannon Clarkson, eds., *Dictionary of Feminist Theologies* (Louisville: Westminster John Knox Press, 1996), 151–52; and Daniel L. Migliore, *Faith Seeking Understanding: An Introduction to Christian Theology* (Grand Rapids: Eerdmans, 1991), 145–51.

that God has always been present and has often appeared in the flesh. The influence of Greek metaphysical philosophy made a problem out of God's body, and incarnation was the doctrine to overcome this problem.

In Jesus, Christian tradition has claimed that God was present in a special, unique way. Since Jesus' time, the church's theology has struggled to define and explain exactly what happened in Jesus. Some theologies and traditions argue that Jesus was purely human and purely divine, somehow both God and human.[2] Many other explanations exist as well.

In the stories told at Christmas and throughout the gospels and their echoes in other parts of the New Testament, God's presence and nearness become apparent in Jesus, and more of God's image is seen than we may notice anywhere else. The story of God's being with humans, with us, reverberates throughout the ages and affects lives yet today. Emmanuel, God with us, moves off the pages of the text into living belief each day.

To understand Jesus does not require consent to the speculative philosophical arguments about Jesus' nature. Instead, understanding Jesus begins with hearing the story and meeting Jesus. But the story is always one that is repeated; we do not hear it for the first time, and it is not Jesus who tells this story himself. Instead, we hear it through others. Just as we see God through others who follow and reflect God, we hear of Jesus through others who have heard of Jesus, and together we join in hearing, echoing, and repeating the story. These echoes do not sound the same every time; they take on some of the tones of those whose voices make the story come alive. The incarnation of God in Jesus is a story that lives on in the bodies of those who tell the story even this day. Because human life is a difficult experience full of brokenness, it is not surprising that the stories of Jesus begin in that same brokenness.

Beginnings in Brokenness

Each of the four gospels tells a different story of Jesus, or even tells the story of a different Jesus. Certainly, they differ from each

---

[2] For a discussion and critique of the early church's philosophical struggle with incarnation as God's descent into the human, historical world in the form of Jesus, who was God and human, see David W. Odell-Scott, *A Post-Patriarchal Christology*, American Academy of Religion Academy Series 78 (Atlanta: Scholars Press, 1991), 76–83.

other in their understandings of what happened in Jesus and what God was doing in and through Jesus. The differences mean that we need to take each of the four gospels on their own terms, to listen to their own story.

John

The gospel of John is the last of the four gospels in canonical order and the last to be written. Its christology is the most developed, most complex, and most poetic of the four canonical gospels. It begins with a poem that is an ode to the Word.

> In the beginning was the Word, and the Word was with God, and the Word was God.
>
> ....
>
> And the Word became flesh and lived among us, and we have seen his glory, the glory as of a father's only son, full of grace and truth. (John 1:1, 14)

Christian tradition has understood this Word as Jesus, the only son of God the father. Scholars have often connected this to ancient wisdom traditions that presented the Word as a manifestation of God, perhaps like Wisdom was personified in the book of Proverbs and in other wisdom literature from the Israelite tradition. Whether or not this full connection is valid, the gospel of John clearly begins with a metaphysical poem that ties the events of Jesus' life into cosmic history. The Word existed from the beginning, and in Jesus the Word is made flesh in order to live among God's people in glorious fashion. Jesus is the Word made flesh. Jesus is God incarnate, the very embodiment of God in ways that are visible, so that we may behold God's glory, grace, and truth.

God lives in Jesus, and through the events of Jesus, God lives among humans for a time, choosing an embodied, enfleshed existence that is like humanity and that is in humanity's midst. The Greek word that is translated as "lived" among us does not mean simply having life, but more specifically that God dwelled with us. A related word in Greek is the word for "tent." God pitched a tent in our midst and lived inside skin for that time with us. God moves in next door, just down the street. John's gospel echoes the images of Ezekiel and other prophets, envisioning a God whose dwelling place is nearby and whose house is close at hand. In Jesus, God resides with us.

For John, incarnation no longer means God's being with us in the body; it means God's taking a human body to live as one of us. Although the gospel of John offers this metaphysical and poetic interpretation, it is lacking in details of how God accomplishes this incarnation and how others respond to it. The other gospels offer divergent views about what exactly happened in the event of Jesus' birth.

Mark

At first glance, Mark says nothing at all about God's incarnation in Jesus. Certainly, Mark does not talk about Jesus' birth. Instead, the story launches immediately into John the Baptist, who served as a precursor for Jesus, echoing some verses from Isaiah. Mark seems not to see any value in telling a story of Jesus' birth or origins. Mark is much more concerned with what happens in Jesus' ministry than in anything prior, and Mark never dwells for long in any metaphysical speculation. The nature of God and the origin of Jesus could never be as important as the magnificent things that God has done in the world. However, Mark tells a story of Jesus' baptism that in some ways is like a birth story.

> In those days Jesus came from Nazareth of Galilee and was baptized by John in the Jordan. And just as he was coming up out of the water, he saw the heavens torn apart and the Spirit descending like a dove on him. And a voice came from heaven, "You are my son, the beloved; with you I am well pleased." (Mark 1:9–11)

God names Jesus as God's own son. For Mark, this is the beginning of God's work in Jesus, and nothing that went on before matters at all. There is no metaphysical incarnation of a disembodied God into the flesh of Jesus at birth. At baptism, the spirit descends on Jesus, and after that God's voice from heaven pronounces Jesus as God's son. This term, "son of God," is clearly important to Mark, so much that at Jesus' death on the cross, a Roman soldier declares that he believes that Jesus was God's son (Mark 15:39).

Mark never claims that Jesus' role or identity or nature as God's son implies anything genetic or that Jesus and God are one and the same. Mark does not claim that Jesus is God in human flesh. God's spirit is with Jesus, and God loves Jesus, but the gospel of Mark does not claim that God walked the earth in Jesus' flesh. At baptism, Jesus becomes God's son. Many theologians throughout history have likened this to adoption. Jesus is God's son and is part of God's family, but that does not mean that God shares essence, nature, or DNA with Jesus.

Matthew

Matthew's gospel begins with sixteen verses of genealogy, tracing forty-two generations from Abraham to Jesus. This emphasizes Jesus' humanity and his connections to God's people. Jesus' genealogy is a list of faithful persons, a list of marginalized and rejected persons, and a list of sinners, all at once. Matthew does not attempt to cover this up; the gospel almost relishes the chance to remind the reader of all these things of the past.

What God does in Jesus is an act of great scope and power, but it is also an act that is scandalous, edgy, and discomforting. Parentage is frequently difficult to determine or uncomfortable to face. Jesus partakes of all of this within his very ancestry. This is a story of an extremely human Jesus, with a family tree of heroes and villains, not unlike any of ours.

Immediately after the genealogy, the gospel tells the story of Joseph, Jesus' father, who was visited by an angel to announce the upcoming birth of Jesus (Matt. 1:18–25). Joseph and Mary had been engaged to each other but were not yet living together. Church tradition has struggled to interpret this passage to prove Jesus' divinity instead of Jesus' humanity in two different ways. First, Joseph's role has been diminished. Most interpreters have believed that he is not the genetic father of Jesus. Second, Mary's own role as Jesus' mother has been stretched out of normal proportions. Even when tradition agrees that she is a biological mother for Jesus, it argues that she did not become a mother in any human way. Her role becomes wholly passive. She does not do a thing; she engages in no sexual activity; she merely is recipient and temporary bearer of the child God desires. Yet the text of Matthew consistently falls short of all these claims.

Joseph and Mary had been engaged to each other. Their marriage was promised and perhaps even scheduled. Certainly, it was public knowledge. In their culture, it was likely that they were sexually active, even though Mary had not yet moved out of her father's household to Joseph's. Matthew does not insist or suggest that Mary and Joseph had never had sex. Instead, there is merely the statement that they were not living together, which is very different. Joseph does see the pregnancy as a disgrace. He considers calling off the marriage entirely because some people might think he was not the father.

Twice Matthew states that Mary is pregnant by the Holy Spirit. This does not necessarily mean that the spirit had impregnated Mary through sex. People in this culture knew that children came from the sexual union of a woman and a man, but they also knew that there was great mystery about which sexual occasions would lead to pregnancy. They believed that God's spirit (or some other deity, spirit, or mystical agent) opened the womb to allow pregnancy—but that does not mean that they thought women could get pregnant without sex with a man. Matthew emphasizes that Mary's pregnancy is the will of God. The child is not an accident. Although Joseph did not desire this pregnancy and Mary reacts with surprise, God wanted the child and intended the pregnancy.

Matthew, at any one of several points, could easily have stated that Joseph was not the father, or that Mary had never had sex before this, or some other clear, unambiguous assertion. Matthew never makes such a statement.

The angel does quote a passage from Isaiah that tradition has translated as "a virgin shall conceive" and that the son will be named Emmanuel (Matt. 1:23; cf. Isa. 7:14). This has been taken as proof that Mary had never had sex before Jesus was born. However, the Isaiah passage, as well as Greek society in Mary and Joseph's day, did not define the word used here (*betulah* in Hebrew; *parthenos* in Greek) as a woman who had never had sex, but as a woman who had never birthed a child.[3] We should not think of the woman in Isaiah's prophecy, or of Mary, as a virgin in our cultural terms, but as a young woman. Matthew's clearest statement is that Joseph did not have sex with Mary after the angel's visit until the birth of Jesus. The rest of Joseph and Mary's sex life is not told to the reader.

Thus, the genealogy and the story of Joseph's visit with an angel begin the story of Jesus with two different perspectives that make the same point. Jesus' beginnings were normal. From Abraham on, one generation leads to another in the normal human fashion of pregnancy and childbirth. But this is also spectacular. An angel announces the birth. This is a child that God wants and intends.

---

[3] It should also be noted that the boy Jesus does not have the name Emmanuel. The Isaiah prophecy may be fulfilled, but not in a way that takes a literal replication of the words.

Matthew does not suggest that Jesus is the embodiment of God. Matthew's gospel does not even propose that anyone but Joseph and Mary are Jesus' natural parents. Instead, Matthew's story presents Jesus as a child born by natural processes and God's desire. Jesus is the son that God wants Joseph and Mary to have and to raise. God wants that boy, and Jesus is no accident at all.

Luke

For the gospel of Luke, the story of Jesus' beginnings encompasses much more. Luke begins with Zechariah and Elizabeth, an aging priest and his wife, who was also from a priestly family (Luke 1:5–7). An angel appeared to Zechariah and announced that he and Elizabeth would have a child. In Luke, angels and miraculous births appear even before Jesus. The child John will be filled with the Holy Spirit even before birth (Luke 1:15).

Only after this does an angel appear to Mary (Luke 1:26–37). There are several key differences between this account and the one in Matthew. In Matthew, the angel appeared to Joseph after Mary was pregnant. In Luke, Mary receives the visit from the angel Gabriel before her conception. Joseph talked with the visiting angel about something that had already happened and about his reaction to what Mary had done and what the community would think. In Matthew, Mary is identified through the Isaiah passage as a young woman and by the narrator as an engaged woman not yet living with her fiancé. Luke portrays Mary as a young engaged woman (Luke 1:27) who is not yet pregnant (Luke 1:31) and who tells the angel that she has never had sex with a man before (Luke 1:34).[4]

Luke surrounds Mary's pregnancy and birthing with the sounds of praise. John, the unborn child inside Elizabeth, leaps for joy (Luke 1:41, 44), and Elizabeth is filled with the Holy Spirit (Luke 1:41). Mary offers a song of praise in response (Luke 1:46–55). Zechariah, Elizabeth's husband, also praises God (Luke 1:64, 67–79). When Jesus is born, angels and shepherds praise God (Luke 2:8–20), and at his circumcision, the temple priest Simeon also praises God (Luke 2:25–32), along with Anna, a temple prophet (Luke 2:38).

Although the gospel of Luke begins with clarity on Jesus' special relationship with God, which is a cause for great praise and joy, the

---

[4] The Greek says literally, "I have never known a man." Mary claims she never had sex. The NRSV translates this as "I am a virgin," but the word *parthenos* does not appear here.

gospel's beginnings do not describe or analyze what makes Jesus special. It is not yet known what it means to be the son of God. The later chapters of all the gospels explore that idea by examining Jesus' life. The answer is not in Jesus' origins at all.

The Meaning of Jesus' Birth

For most of the church's tradition, the meaning of Jesus' birth has been that God came to live among humans. Before Jesus, God was distant and heavenly. In Jesus, God came close and became human, living on the earth, still fully God but also fully human. However, this is not what the gospels emphasize. In fact, this direction of thinking about Jesus' birth assumes that God was not living among humans before, but the Old Testament and the gospels portray God as intimately involved and physically present throughout history. If God was never absent, then God does not *become* present in Jesus—even though Jesus is one of the ways that God is present in the world.

The gospels themselves claim that Jesus is the Son of God, but not that Jesus is God or embodies God in that kind of way. The Old and New Testaments contain many references to God's children, and Jesus is one of them. Jesus' role as God's son is not what makes Jesus unique. However, it does point to Jesus as an incarnation and embodiment of God, along with all the other people throughout history through whom people can see the image of God in clear and fresh ways.

Although the gospels do not support the metaphysical idea of God's taking on human flesh one time only in Jesus, the gospels clearly point out that there is something special happening in the birth and life of Jesus. There is a sense in which God is more visible in Jesus than anywhere else. In Jesus' words, God's voice rings out. When Jesus is known, people feel joy and break forth in beautiful expressions of praise. The reality of God is felt to be near in Jesus' presence. Wherever Jesus is, God is there. Of course, God has been present among God's people in so many ways for so long, that this should not be surprising, yet the experience of God's presence always does surprise. The daily human experience is much more focused on God's absence, for God is the one for whom we long and whom we desire. We know that God is visible and present, but we have a difficult time sensing God in the midst of our lives. We long for the moment when we can see God face-to-face. For some reason, perhaps a reason that will remain forever unexplainable, people in Jesus' day and even long afterward looked at Jesus and felt God's presence. They saw God face-to-face in this human son of God. Because they saw God in Jesus, the people of Jesus' day reacted to God in their midst. God had always been with them, in so many ways, but in Jesus' presence, they felt God at hand.

In all of life, God is present. In Jesus' presence, many people felt God's presence, perhaps for the first time in their lives. It was as if God, who had always been there, was suddenly visible, hearable, touch-able, graspable. It was as if God had been born in their midst. In the midst of this world with its wonders and its harshness, God lived in Jesus. What would happen if God were born as a human, to live a human life, to experience human existence, and to interact with hu-mans just as the rest of us do? In Jesus, the question finds an answer.

The Birth of God in a Murderous World

God's presence in Jesus requires risk. Some people respond to God's presence in Jesus with praise. Others respond less favorably. Angels, shepherds, sages, and distant relatives combine to sing the praises of God at Jesus' birth. Others feel fear, and fear breeds hatred. Matthew's story of the wise men's visit to Jesus provides a good ex-ample of these mixed responses to God's incarnation in Jesus. At Christmas pageants and within the church's faith, we usually concen-trate on how the story ends with praise (Matt. 2:9–12). But the story is mostly about Herod (Matt. 2:1–8). Herod feared Jesus, and his response to Jesus had a chilling end: He slaughtered untold numbers of innocent children (Matt. 2:16–18). The result of his fear at Jesus' birth was a massacre of children, echoing throughout the people in wailing, lamentation, and weeping, without consolation.

After Jesus' baptism, he went into the wilderness for forty days of prayer and fasting. Then the devil appeared to tempt Jesus with three tests: food in exchange for a self-serving display of ability, power in exchange for subservience, and protection in time of self-afflicted en-dangerment (Matt. 4:1–11; Mark 1:12–13; Luke 4:1–13). In each case, Jesus declined the devil's offers, quoting ancient Israel's scriptures.

The spiritual powers of the world also opposed God's incarna-tion. In the gospels' worldview, the political powers fought with de-cree and genocide, but the spiritual powers of the world struggled against God in Jesus with more subtle persuasions. The devil did not seek to kill Jesus, but merely suggested paths of action that would lessen God's own being. The reaction against God's incarnation from one side is to squelch God, from the other side to corrupt. All around Jesus are those who would co-opt the power of God and diminish the autonomy of God in the flesh.

Throughout the gospels, the reader finds Jesus' own pronouncements that his death at the hands of the people's leaders is inevitable (Mark 10:32–34). As Jesus' ministry progressed, the number of people allied against him only increased. Jesus would be betrayed. The leaders would decide to execute him. The Roman government would concur and would put him to death. The execution would be vile, disgusting, and degrading. The gospels tell that Jesus promised he would rise up after that, but the disciples never knew what that meant.

Herod's action against Jesus when Jesus was still an infant was only the beginning. Throughout Jesus' life, he made enemies, and those enemies were powerful persons who began to plot Jesus' death.

In the gospel of John, the opposition against Jesus occurs on a more popular level. Early in Jesus' teaching, those who are listening to him begin to complain among themselves because Jesus' words were very hard for them to accept (John 6:60–61). Many of the disciples stop following Jesus at this point (John 6:66), and the gospel recounts that not even Jesus' own brothers believe in him (John 7:5). The people who throng to listen to Jesus argue among themselves about who he is (John 7:40–43). Before long, Jesus' public appearances often end in the masses' taking up stones to kill him (John 10:31), even while the authorities are seeking to arrest him (John 10:39). When Jesus' powerful signs encourage people to believe in him, the tide turns, and the rulers plot to kill Jesus themselves (John 11:53).

Although the rulers plan to execute Jesus, the everyday people who hear Jesus turn against him first. God's voice in Jesus is offensive and difficult. Eventually the people pick up stones to murder Jesus themselves. The gospel of John weaves Jesus' story between the threads of those who would oppose what God is doing in the flesh. Jesus is hard pressed on every side, with opponents everywhere. Not even the disciples believe Jesus all the time, and one of them is the betrayer. Yet God is present in Jesus, and God's embodied activity continues.

How to Understand the Impossible

Almost all the characters in the canonical gospels sense that something special is happening in Jesus. The problem in explaining Jesus is an inevitable difficulty in explaining the inexplicable and the impossible. In the philosophical thought of the Greek and Roman worlds in New Testament times, God was infinite and was spirit, an essence of pure being. Humans were finite, limited, and bounded; human life was a reality of flesh and bodied actions. God and human were completely incompatible categories, according to many ways of thinking. The idea that the infinite God could be in the human Jesus made no sense at all to these schools of thought.

The gospels found the Old Testament, especially Isaiah, to be helpful in their attempt to explain Jesus.[5] They wished to put the events of Jesus, events that they understood to be unique and as outside the framework of previous human experience, into words that everyone could understand. They put the inexpressible into words by referring to words of the past, words that were already known, familiar, and understood. They tried to explain the inexplicable in terms of what was already explained and comprehended.

The Sign of Immanuel

Isaiah was a prophet in Jerusalem in the days when Judah was a kingdom of its own, with Ahaz as its king. There were wars and rumors of wars in the land. Alliances were shifting among Judah's neighbors. Isaiah told Ahaz not to enter into any of the factions, but instead to wait out the conflict.

But Ahaz found this advice very difficult to hear, and he did not want to listen to Isaiah and his prophecies at all. Isaiah challenged Ahaz to request a sign from God. When Ahaz refused, Isaiah offered his own sign.

Therefore the Lord will give you a sign. Look, the young woman is with child and shall bear a son, and shall name

---

[5]For an extensive discussion of how the New Testament uses Old Testament images to describe Jesus, see Frederick C. Holmgren, *The Old Testament and the Significance of Jesus: Embracing Change—Maintaining Christian Identity* (Grand Rapids: Eerdmans, 1999), especially the list on 142.

him Immanuel. He shall eat curds and honey by the time he knows how to refuse the evil and choose the good. For before the child knows how to refuse the evil and choose the good, the land before whose two kings you are in dread will be deserted. (Isa. 7:14–16)

Within the context of Ahaz and Isaiah, this sign refers to the birth of a child. Isaiah stood before Ahaz within the royal court, and he pointed to one of the young women in their presence. This woman would have been one of the wives or concubines of the king, because the king owned and controlled all the people within his presence. Isaiah singled out one woman and told Ahaz and the court that she was pregnant. Isaiah predicted that the child would be a boy and directed that the king name his son Immanuel, which means "God is with us." The unrequested sign that Isaiah offered to Ahaz is to be Ahaz's own son, the heir to the throne. This may well be the son named Hezekiah, who would become king after Ahaz.[6] Whenever Ahaz saw his son Hezekiah, he would be reminded of the sign from God. Isaiah interpreted what the sign would mean. Before little Immanuel was old enough to tell wrong from right, the battling nations that Ahaz feared would all be destroyed and Judah would be wealthy enough to eat fine foods such as curds and honey. With the enemies vanquished, Judah would live some of its best days ever; peace and prosperity would arrive together, and it would all happen within the first few years of this little boy in the womb of the woman standing nearby in the king's court.

The sign of Immanuel, then, is a reminder that God's future is just at hand. But there is a natural, unassuming, gradual way to this sign. The birth of Immanuel does not require miracles in the heavens. It is the way of all flesh, the cycle of life that all share. Immanuel is a sign for everyone, a notification from God that God's physical presence is as simple as a newborn baby.

In Matthew's gospel, an angel quotes this prophecy of Immanuel to Joseph when announcing that Mary is pregnant (Matt. 1:23). Then Joseph begins to understand what the boy Jesus will mean. God's presence is surprising, irresistible, uncontrollable, and an unspeakable blessing. The future of a child is always known—the child lives

---

[6]Note that in both this prophetic naming of an unborn son and in that of Jesus, the name Immanuel is predicted but is never used to name the child.

and dies, according to the way of all flesh. Yet the details that the child lives out each day take on so many different forms that each day is a new adventure, with its end never predictable. Such is life with God, and such is the way that God appears in Jesus.

A Child Shall Lead Them

The story of Hezekiah, Ahaz's son, does not end with the reference to his birth. The early chapters of Isaiah are full of the expectations of what the world can be when young Hezekiah takes the throne and rules Judah in the way that God intends. Isaiah offers a beautiful hymn that portrays a day of liberation and freedom after the afflictions of war (Isa. 9:2–7). A young child will become king after a brutal conflict, and in the days when this boy Hezekiah rules, there will be endless peace, based on justice and righteousness for the whole people. In Isaiah's day, this may well have been what the prophet hoped would happen in the near future, when Hezekiah took the throne. The anticipation was high, but if Isaiah was right about the politics of his time, unprecedented prosperity and a lasting peace were just around the corner.

Because the people were so dependent upon the king, they recognized that their own welfare was at stake when a new heir to the kingdom was born or when a new king took the throne. It made sense for them to think that a prince meant "a child has been born for us, a son given to us." They knew that the prince would affect them and change their lives just as adding to their own family would.

Isaiah depicts the way that Hezekiah would rule as one of peace and of blissful cooperation within the world of nature (Isa. 11:1–9). When everyone knows God, there will be peace at the most basic levels within the world. Long-lasting enmities will cease, and age-old enemies will cooperate together. In this peaceful world, the very nature of the animals will change in order to make peace within the world. Snakes will not bite; bears and lions will become vegetarians; prey and predator will abandon the roles they have learned and lived from birth and will find other ways to be in the world. A little child will lead them all into new ways of life. With righteousness, this child will make the right decisions to help the poor and the disadvantaged of the earth, protecting them by vanquishing the wicked.

This vision of God's new world is the same as what God is doing in Jesus. Jesus' activity does not start with the top strata of society;

instead, he lives among the disadvantaged and begins to include them in the growing reality of God (Luke 1:51–53; cf. 1 Sam. 2:1–10). This is a reversal of fortunes, a change as fundamental as when lions become safe bedmates for calves and fatlings.

When God's intentions for human life become manifest, whether in the life of Hezekiah or of Jesus, things will change. God's new society will have different values, and different people will be lifted up and exalted. The appearance of the child is just the beginning, but it is a beginning that marks the inevitability of God's intentions for a different way of human life.

God's Spirit and the Anointed One

When Jesus speaks in the gospels to describe his own work, his words echo a later part of Isaiah.

> The spirit of the Lord GOD is upon me,
>> because the LORD has anointed me;
> he has sent me to bring good news to the oppressed,
>> to bind up the brokenhearted,
>> to proclaim liberty to the captives,
>>> and release to the prisoners;
>> to proclaim the year of the LORD's favor,
>>> and the day of vengeance of our God;
>> to comfort all who mourn;
>> to provide for those who mourn in Zion —
>>> to give them a garland instead of ashes,
>>> the oil of gladness instead of mourning,
>>> the mantle of praise instead of a faint spirit.
> They will be called oaks of righteousness,
>> the planting of the LORD, to display his glory.
> They shall build up the ancient ruins,
>> they shall raise up the former devastations;
> they shall repair the ruined cities,
>> the devastations of many generations.
>> (Isa. 61:1–4; cf. Luke 4:16–21)

In quoting this passage, Jesus offers one of the clearest explanations of how he sees his own role. When he follows his reading of the Isaiah passage with his provocative statement, "Today this scripture has been fulfilled in your hearing," he claims God's spirit in order to undertake this ministry (Luke 4:21). The mourning of God's people will turn to gladness and joy. Jesus proclaims that this is the time of God's favor; God will act on behalf of all hurting people. God's will becomes evident, visible, and palpable in the world through God's activities as announced and begun by Jesus.

But in quoting this passage, Jesus also points beyond his own role. The Jews in the synagogue who heard Jesus would have known that God always acts toward these goals. Jesus does not claim a special role for himself; instead, he indicates what God has always done in the world. What God does in Jesus is important, but it is not new. This is what God always does.

Explaining the Impossible

Church tradition developed many different doctrines to explain how Jesus was unique, such as the idea that God was physically embodied in Jesus, or that God and Jesus were of the same essence, or that God had impregnated the Virgin Mary. However, the gospels avoid these philosophical speculations as they try to understand Jesus, preferring instead the concepts of Isaiah.

Jesus was like Immanuel, the child called Hezekiah, the son of Ahaz. Jesus was a sign that God was present with the people and that God's involvement would soon bring about a magnificent new era of peace and prosperity for the people, no matter how difficult things might seem at the moment. Oppression of all sorts would end in this new way of life that God is about to bring to God's people. This reign of God will grow and keep growing, and nothing will be able to stand in its way as it brings justice to those who are near and to those who are far away at the distant ends of the earth. God's reign will come gently yet persistently; it will not appear in a sudden blaze of glory, but as the softest of winds, yet strong enough to change everything, eventually. In Jesus, God was bringing about a time of peace that would change the very nature of those in God's creation, making vegetarians out of the wildest beasts so that they could live peaceably with the animals that they used to eat as prey. This is a miraculous reversal of nature. The old impulses to harm and destroy will wither away as new priorities of love and care, justice and righteousness, and comfort and transformation take over within human life. Jesus is the one anointed by God's spirit to begin all these changes.

But Jesus' own description of his work, taken from Isaiah 61, is not that Jesus *causes* these changes in human life brought about by the reign of God, but that Jesus *announces* them. Jesus announces God's vision for the world, which is the same vision that God set forth at creation and to which God has called God's people throughout all times and places.

Responding to the Impossible

The beginnings of the gospels concentrate not so much on how to understand Jesus as God's physical embodied presence as on showing the ways that various people and powers responded to the presence of Jesus in their midst.

One of the first responses—and plainly one of the least subtle—was to kill Jesus. This was Herod's response (Matt. 2:1–18). As king, he felt that this infant was a threat and so he arranged the massacre of an untold number of baby boys, just to make sure that Jesus died among the whole group of them. The drive to murder Jesus and to eliminate the physical presence of God was repeated throughout Jesus' life, all the way to the crucifixion of Jesus. One of the most frequent responses to God's presence in Jesus was to kill Jesus and, perhaps in so doing, to kill God.

The temptation scenes in the gospels present a second response (Matt. 4:1–11; Mark 1:12–13; Luke 4:1–13). In these stories, Satan tempts Jesus to give up the agenda of God and to find other goals. The impulse to corrupt Jesus and to reduce God to a servant endures throughout the gospels. The disciples often felt that they knew better than Jesus did about the direction that his ministry should take. They had ideas about how God's reign would arrive and how it should be organized, but their suggestions were self-serving. Many of the people's leaders met with Jesus, in public or in private, with their own willingness to embrace Jesus as long as he did not disrupt their plans. Jesus consistently resisted these attempts at seduction and corruption.

A more subtle response to the impossibility of explaining and understanding Jesus' presence was to try to transform Jesus into an object of worship. The clearest case of this in the gospels comes at one of the most inexplicable moments: the transfiguration, when Jesus appears glorified with Moses and Elijah next to him (Matt. 17:1–8; Mark 9:2–8; Luke 9:28–36). In response to this miraculous appearance, Peter suggests that they erect a shrine to the occasion.

Then Peter said to Jesus, "Rabbi, it is good for us to be here; let us make three dwellings, one for you, one for Moses, and one for Elijah."

He did not know what to say, for they were terrified. (Mark 9:5–6)

The desire to worship Jesus occurred in Jesus' life, and he rebuffed it whenever it happened. In years since, however, Jesus has become an object to be worshiped, despite the record of Jesus' own words and actions against such things. Peter rightly noticed how miraculous the transfiguration was, but his response was wrong. Peter tried to enshrine Jesus and worship Jesus, and the gospels do not support such responses.

If Jesus becomes an object in a shrine, then those who operate the shrine and define the right worship have co-opted Jesus into their agenda. Placing Jesus in a shrine is a subtle form of corruption, for it ends Jesus' activity in the task of announcing a new world. Jesus' own speech stops as soon as he becomes the object of devotion. An enshrined Jesus has no followers, only worshipers. God asks for followers, which means that God—and thus Jesus—must keep moving, even if their movement is unpredictable. Those who would be with Jesus must pay attention and must follow; no one can count on Jesus' remaining static. God in Jesus stays free, even free from the shackles and objectification of being worshiped.

Whatever God was doing in Jesus, it is not to result in worship. We must not make Jesus into an object for our devotion and dedication. Accepting worship was one of Jesus' temptations. He resisted because we should worship only God, not anyone else, not even Jesus. We must remain in pursuit of the God who would have us follow. Just as no tomb of death can hold back God's presence in Jesus, neither can any shrine.

Enshrining and worshiping Jesus can take many forms. Constructing physical temples, whether elaborate shrines or simple tents on hilltops, is only part of it. The modern world is full of systems of thought that define and restrain Jesus. The theological systems that serve to explain and predict Jesus are also attempts to limit the unpredictability of God in Jesus. We want to understand God and Jesus, so we make our beliefs into systems of thought that claim to know God's will. It is like capturing the wind, or at least claiming foolishly that we can understand and predict it. We can feel the wind; we can know its direction; and maybe we can point to it when it passes. But we cannot predict it. If we capture it to study it, it is no longer the wind. If we construct theories about God, we have lost the very unpredictability of God. We cease knowing God; we only know our theories about God.

Worship and theology are two responses to God's presence in Jesus that the gospels themselves do not support. Instead, the gospels are resistant to any deification of Jesus or any domestication of God into doctrine. We have taken the inexplicable presence of God in Jesus and domesticated it, turning God into assertions and propositions that we can analyze for our own privilege. We can discern our own most prudent course of action, and we can differentiate ourselves from those whose beliefs do not measure up to the criteria and norms of our theological systems. In all this activity, we have lost the point and have forsaken a relationship with the living God who was present in Jesus.

The gospels encourage us to resist the wrong responses and instead to join those who praise and celebrate what God announces in Jesus. Mary and Joseph, Zechariah and Elizabeth, and sages and shepherds all from the beginning recognize in Jesus a reason for celebration. God's presence in Jesus is a cause for joy. Of course, there has always been reason for praise in God's presence (Ps. 150).

God's presence in Jesus may be impossible to explain, but God is present every day. God is always present with us, even though we cannot explain or analyze that presence of relationship. Every day is reason for celebration. God's presence in Jesus is no more or less understandable than God's presence in any other way, whether in body in the garden of Eden or by image or voice to the ancients or to those of us today. We may never know why God loves us. We may not know how to categorize and analyze that love. It remains unpredictable, perhaps frightening, certainly destabilizing, maybe threatening. It takes courage to respond without striking out to kill, or struggling to wrestle God into accepting our priorities, or enshrining Jesus in a static place of our own choosing. But to respond fully to God's presence in Jesus is not an act of comprehension or of control, but of celebration of the infinite ways in which God is present in Jesus and in every other way.

The impossible happens every day that God is with us, whether in Jesus or in any other way. God's presence in relationship means that we can respond with joy. We do not know the reasons why or mechanisms by which God is present with us, but we know a wonderful relationship as Jesus announced it. We do not know why; we know God, in Jesus.

6

EMBODIED MINISTRY

When Jesus walked among humanity, God was in our midst. Although the mechanics of God's presence remains beyond human explanation, the experience of God allows a relationship to begin. God had always been present, but many people did not notice until Jesus. With all the ways that God has been present in Jesus and in so many other experiences before and since, Jesus remains the way of seeing God's physical presence that for Christians most often begins the relationship.

The beginning of relationships can be very difficult. In fact, many relationships with wonderful potential never get past the first few awkward steps. Things can go wrong in so many ways. We may never meet, or the introduction may go clumsily, or missed phone calls may signal a lack of interest. A silence in a conversation or an unintentionally offensive phrase can cause everyone to rethink whether or not to continue getting to know each other. In those first moments and early days of a relationship, numerous incidents can derail even the most promising connections.

Once we start to get to know each other, the difficulties are not over. There are many responses to someone's interest and self-disclosure that can turn a relationship from a promising possibility to a nightmare. Perhaps someone moves too quickly, or another too slowly. In Jesus' case, the responses included subtle attempts to define who Jesus was and domesticate God's presence into something safe and enshrined so that Jesus could be an object of worship and devotion. There were also those who wished to corrupt Jesus more openly into accepting other agendas and giving up God's own ineffable independence. Some even wished to kill Jesus in response to God's presence among us. All these responses occurred. But there were also right responses to the beginnings of God with us in Jesus. The right responses were celebration, joy, and praise. Just as in any relationship, the best foundation for knowing each other is not an attempt to destroy, corrupt, control, or idolize the other, but instead to enjoy the sheer otherness of a new friend or love. So many of the people who first knew Jesus broke forth in song, their hearts full of the music that communicates the joy of new love.

For those who know the love of Jesus and the depth of relationship with God, those marvelous days of first getting to know each other still ring in our ears like sweet melody, like the tunes that we cannot get out of our minds, so we hum them to ourselves over and over. We are like lovers reliving those early romantic moments when everything was possibility. We celebrate those times.

But love grows and matures. Anything else is idolatry, the staticness of being enshrined as someone else's object of love instead of growing into the fullness of relationship. It is good to remember the old days when love was new and fresh, but we must not let those memories, as exciting and intoxicating as they are, distract us permanently from the ways that our relationships change over time. Beginnings are important, but they are only beginnings.

After beginnings come deepening a relationship and getting to know each other at new levels. It means learning each other's quirks and habits, dreams and desires, and wishes and worries. This period in a relationship involves a lot of watching and listening to observe each other and find out what the other is really like, not only on the surface but also in the midst of all of life's less attractive moments. So there is careful listening, trying to hear what is said and not said, as well as close watching, maybe even staring into each other's eyes, to see what is really going on in a person's life and mind. But this careful observation is a process not only of being in love but also of finding out about one's self. Some of this is developing shared tastes and habits, trying new things together and learning how to appreciate things with someone who is passionate about them. But something deeper is going on with this. Loving another means loving and discovering one's self; there is no healthy way to separate those. It is like staring into the other's eyes long enough to see one's own reflection, or it is like learning to see one's self through someone else's eyes entirely. Through the eyes of friends and lovers, we see ourselves as we really are: wonderful, flawed, and loved.

In the same way, life with Jesus is a process of learning about God. Through watching Jesus carefully over the span of years, we begin to discern more and more about who God is and what God is like to live with. We also begin to become a bit more like God and to understand ourselves better, both who we are and who we can be. The gospels indicate that Jesus participates in the same process, for Jesus is in this relationship as well. Together, Jesus and those around him learn to live together and to love each other, and at the same time they learn about each other and about themselves.

By watching Jesus in the gospels, we today can learn about this relationship with God. We learn about who God is and what God is like through watching Jesus and what he does in the stories of the gospels. In Jesus, God took on an embodied presence in the midst of human beings. The ministry of Jesus, those acts that he performed out of loving relationship, is perhaps the best place to look to understand what it means that God is with us. As important as the beginnings are in shaping a relationship, the adult actions that are taken over time shape it all the more. Jesus' ministry was to announce that God's reign was coming to fill the world with a commitment to justice and a new way of life. This much was clear from the start. But the ways in which Jesus works this out, discovering others and even himself through interactions with people, make much clearer what God is doing in Jesus.

Learning to Live with Jesus

Throughout the gospels are stories of how Jesus would meet people and would interact with them. Each of these people began to understand and to enact how to live life with Jesus and in God's presence.

The impossible presence of God, made real through these encounters with Jesus, could be a transforming experience for those who met him.[1] Throughout the gospels, we read a story of Jesus' life unfolding. The more we read, the more we learn who Jesus was. This is especially true if we read the stories in which Jesus learns about his own ministry through his interactions with others.

In the gospel of John appears a story about Jesus when he stopped at a well while traveling through the region of Samaria. While he was resting there, a woman also came to the well. The two of them talked, which may have been unusual in a culture where men and women rarely spoke in public and where Samaritans and Jews were often at odds with each other. Perhaps it was only that Jesus did not have any way to get water out of the well, and the woman who lived nearby had brought a bucket with her. Perhaps it was nothing but necessity that brought the two of them to break the rules of social custom and to speak to each other. Certainly, their opening conversation was perfunctory and none too friendly.

> A Samaritan woman came to draw water, and Jesus said to her, "Give me a drink." (His disciples had gone to the city to buy food.)
>
> The Samaritan woman said to him, "How is it that you, a Jew, ask a drink of me, a woman of Samaria?" (Jews do not share things in common with Samaritans.)
>
> Jesus answered her, "If you knew the gift of God, and who it is that is saying to you, 'Give me a drink,' you would have asked him, and he would have given you living water." (John 4:7–10)

Jesus asked her for help in getting water, and she seemed mystified, skeptical, and perhaps a bit harried by the request. The beginnings of this conversation are quite inauspicious. But Jesus leads the conversation astray. It had been a chat about water, about the physical and embodied needs that all humans share, and about Jesus' own deficiencies—after all, he did not have a bucket, and so a well of water did him no good at all. He needed this woman to help him, or

---

[1]For comments on Jesus as one who models belief, see Clark M. Williamson, *Way of Blessing, Way of Life: A Christian Theology* (St. Louis: Chalice Press, 1999), 214–15.

else his thirst would go unsatisfied. Their relationship began with this recognition of Jesus' own needs as an embodied human. Soon, however, Jesus redirected the conversation from what he needed to who he was.

Jesus did not quite disclose his identity. The woman, on the other hand, expressed many labels for him. At first, she called him a Jew (John 4:9). As the conversation continued, she called him a prophet (John 4:19), and then began to hint that he might be the Messiah before Jesus responded at all.

> The woman said to him, "I know that Messiah is coming" (who is called Christ). "When he comes, he will proclaim all things to us."
>
> Jesus said to her, "I am he, the one who is speaking to you." (John 4:25–26)

Although many English translations report that Jesus said, "I am he," meaning that Jesus claims to be the Messiah, this overrepresents what the passage itself says. The woman talks about the Messiah, and Jesus responds with his only claim in this passage, but it is a very plain sense of identity: "I am the person who is speaking to you." There is no grand messianic vision, no identification with God at a metaphysical level. All that Jesus claims is that he is speaking to the woman. That alone is miracle enough. He broke the social conventions in order to speak honestly and openly with a Samaritan woman about the worship of God. Future miracles were not needed after this one very human contact around a well.

Later the people who come to see Jesus proclaim him as savior of the world (John 4:42). Jesus' identity is not something that he forces on others; it is a realization that comes out of the discussion that he has with other people. They experience that there is something special about Jesus, and they grope for words—messiah, prophet, savior. But the words are never as important as the presence of God in their midst and the chance to worship the God whose presence touches them in conversations with Jesus.

The conversation between Jesus and the Samaritan woman at the well had a tense beginning as they bantered. Although many of Jesus' meetings with people went more smoothly, others were even more contentious. The gospel of Mark tells the story of Jesus and a woman from the Mediterranean coast, northwest of Judea (Mark 7:24–30). The story begins with Jesus being intentionally reclusive, a theme that recurs throughout Mark. Even though Jesus wanted some time by himself and was avoiding contact with anyone who might want something from him, this woman found him and told him the story of how her daughter had contracted an evil spirit, perhaps manifesting itself in some form of life-threatening illness. Jesus' response is far from the compassionate healing words that most gospel readers expect. In fact, Jesus is rude and hostile. He insults the woman and likens her to a dog. Worse, it seems that racist thinking underlies his refusal; the implication is that Jesus' healing should be reserved for Jews and not given to Gentiles.[2] The woman immediately confronts this attitude of Jesus with opposition and sarcasm. She takes Jesus' characterization of herself and her sick daughter as dogs unworthy of Jesus' direct help, and she uses that image to argue with Jesus. She replies that even the dogs under the table can eat the crumbs that children drop there. In response, because she said these words, Jesus heals the daughter at a distance.

Jesus changes his own course of action because of the quick and clever words of this wise woman. She bests Jesus in a verbal duel and wins the healing of her child as a result. In the process, perhaps Jesus begins to change his own thinking about himself and about the people he should help. Because of the interaction, Jesus experiences a transformation of identity; no longer is he simply a healer for Israel but now one whose work announces the day of God's salvation for all people, including Gentiles. This is not a case of Jesus' revealing his identity; he is developing and changing through transforming encounters with others who lead him to do things that he had not thought of doing before he had met these people and talked to them. In the conversations, he changes. Jesus becomes the embodiment of God's announcement of healing and salvation to the whole world.

The gospel of Luke tells of a woman with a debilitating illness. Despite seeking help for this illness for more than a decade, she had not been able to find healing. When Jesus was traveling to meet with

---

[2]The version of the story in Matthew 15:21–28 brings the racial concerns more to the forefront of the text. Mark's story never makes clear what the difference is between children and dogs, but the closeness of this saying to the identification of the woman's geographic origin strongly suggests that the distinction is racial/ethnic.

a religious leader named Jairus, who had a sick daughter, this woman saw Jesus passing by, and she acted by reaching out to him (Luke 8:42b–48). Jesus seemed unaware of what was going on around him, until someone touched him, and he felt something odd within himself. He did not seek out this woman; he did not know her situation; he did not know that she had been healed or what needs she had beforehand; even afterward, Jesus did not seem to know her name or any details about her except for the fact of her faith.

Yet, the woman knew so much of the story. She knew about Jesus and believed that he could help her with only a touch. She sought him and reached out, recognizing her own need and his capability when he seemed unaware of either of them. Her faith made her well. Yet after the healing, Jesus still wanted to speak with her, to learn who she was and what had happened.

In all these stories, Jesus is learning who he is. He hears the labels others give to him: Jew, master, prophet, messiah, savior, healer, powerful one. It is as if Jesus is in a process of figuring out who he is and what he will be doing. He knows that his task is to announce the time of God's favor and the transformation of the world, but Jesus is always searching for ways to connect with people. In these stories, Jesus takes on the roles that address the needs of others, as bit by bit he learns what those needs are. Because the people he meets are embodied just as he is, they have physical needs, and Jesus often responds to the physical needs for healing, as well as meeting people with his own physical needs—the need for water, as well as the need to understand what was happening with his own body when power went out from him. Jesus also deals with needs that are embodied in more than the individual body, such as the need for loving family in the form of healed daughters and accepting communities. In turn, Jesus learns about his own nature and ministry. As with all human relationships, there is give and take, and everyone discovers something about themselves.

In these stories, we can learn about being God's people. It is a slow process of discovery. The knowledge of God does not dawn on us in a single moment; it comes over time through relationships with God and with others. As it develops, we begin to break down the barriers that separate us from one another and that bar the progress of God's reign on earth. Jesus violates the racial divides, the customs that separate men and women, the arrogance that decides what privileges belong to which people, and the rules that keep the healthy away from the sick. Performing the work of God means going beyond those barriers, and in the times when God's people violate those boundaries, we learn something about God and about the life to which God calls us all. In those places, we learn to be like Jesus, to invest ourselves in caring and healing relationships and to live our lives as Jesus lived his: as a sign of what God is doing in the world, made manifest first in bodies like that of Jesus.

The Reason for Incarnation

Jesus' sense of self seems to develop over time through interaction with other people. Because Jesus is human, this is to be expected. The portrait of Jesus in the gospels seems incomplete, or else Jesus is someone who continues daily to discover himself and to reveal himself through his actions, as are all humans.

This way of portraying Jesus may well be intentional. The early church seems to know that Jesus was continually discovering what it meant to be God's servant who would announce God's reign. In the years after Jesus, there were a large number of stories about Jesus. The gospel of John ends with the statement that there have been so many stories about Jesus that all the books in the whole world would not be enough to write them all down (John 21:25). However, very few of these stories about Jesus were recognized by the church as being part of the accepted literature that became the four canonical gospels.

For instance, other gospels contain several stories of Jesus in his youth, and in most of those noncanonical tales, Jesus recognized himself as a miracle worker at a young age. Jesus knew his abilities from birth, it seems, and so had a very precocious childhood as he used his power to transform physical objects as a way to keep out of the kinds of trouble that kids get into. Once he was playing with a bunch of boys on a rooftop when one of them fell off the roof and died. Some of the adults blamed Jesus for pushing the boy off the roof to his death. When Jesus protested his innocence, the adults did not believe him, so Jesus resurrected the boy in order to have him defend Jesus.[3]

---

[3]This is found in one of the apocryphal gospels, called the Infancy Gospel of Thomas, chapter 9. For these and other stories of Jesus as a child and youth, see Robert J. Miller, ed., *The Complete Gospels: Annotated Scholars Version* (Sonoma, Calif.: Polebridge, 1992).

In these other gospels, Jesus knows who he is and what he can do.[4] These seem to portray Jesus as someone with full self-knowledge from the beginning and as someone who does not change and grow over time nearly as much as Jesus does in the four canonical gospels. The only story of Jesus' youth preserved within the canon tells of Jesus' visiting Jerusalem with his parents (Luke 2:42–51). For a while, he was separated from his parents, and they eventually found him in the temple talking about God's will with the scholars and teachers there. His knowledge of God and scripture was amazing to the scholars. However, it was not so amazing that they thought Jesus was God; they found him remarkable and perhaps unique, but like those around Jesus throughout the gospels, they did not find ways to express exactly how and why Jesus was special. These realizations took much more time than just a few hours of discussion in the temple. Still, the only canonical story of Jesus' youth shows him talking and interacting with others. His work proceeds through conversation in which it becomes clearer to himself and to everyone who he is and what he will do.

Within the gospels, one of the pivotal moments is when Jesus asks a very direct question: "Who do you say that I am?" (Matt. 16:13–20; Mark 8:27–30; Luke 9:18–20).

> Jesus went on with his disciples to the villages of Caesarea Philippi; and on the way he asked his disciples, "Who do people say that I am?"
>
> And they answered him, "John the Baptist; and others, Elijah; and still others, one of the prophets."
>
> He asked them, "But who do you say that I am?"
>
> Peter answered him, "You are the Messiah."
>
> And he sternly ordered them not to tell anyone about him. (Mark 8:27–30)

Throughout the church's history, this question has most typically been understood as a challenge or as a test. In this interpretation, Jesus has always known the answer to his own identity, and he chooses

---

[4]Of course, we do not know what Jesus was thinking. In the gospels, we read interpretations of Jesus' thought. We all struggle to understand Jesus, and so we may identify in Jesus the ways he struggled to understand himself through conversation with others.

a particular time to test the disciples to see if they know the truth. The disciples then list some wrong answers: John the Baptist, Elijah, an ancient prophet, a modern-day prophet, or anyone else. Peter, however, has the right answer, which the church has often called the good confession: Jesus is the Messiah in Mark's version of the story; Luke renders it "the Messiah of God"; and Matthew says "the Messiah, the son of the living God." In this interpretation, Peter is the first of the disciples to pass the test of correctly discerning Jesus' true identity.

But what is most clear about Jesus' question is that it is a question. Actually, it is two questions: What are others saying about Jesus, and what do the disciples say about Jesus? When Peter responds, Jesus tells Peter and the rest of the disciples not to tell anybody about Jesus' identity. In a sense, the identity of Jesus is not something that can be told; it cannot be reduced to words that can be believed without experiencing it. Jesus never tells them that he is the Messiah. It is a conclusion that the disciples reach after they see Jesus and live with him. The identity of Jesus forms over time as the disciples and others come to know Jesus through living with him. Peter's naming of Jesus is not the beginning of faith; it is the result of life together with Jesus and the result of following God together.

Jesus' process of working out his identity through interactions with others continues. In Matthew, Jesus has a conversation with Pontius Pilate, who asks him, "Are you the King of the Jews?" To this, Jesus does not answer yes or no. Instead, he replies, "You say so" (Matt. 27:11). Jesus says nothing at all after that. There is nothing left to say. Through interactions with believers and persecutors alike, Jesus' identity has come into formation. Jesus' identity is in flux and in transformation throughout the gospel. Jesus is human like us, and our sense of self is not a static thing that is settled once and for all at birth or at the conclusion of adolescence. Instead, we are always forming our sense of who we are through our interactions with others, friends and enemies alike.

Because identity is built out of interactions with others, Jesus forms an identity through the same process that we do. We learn ourselves in the same way that we learn other people. Through shared life and the togetherness of interaction, we all move toward identity together.

This reverses the claims of traditional theology that God's purpose in Jesus was to attract humans to becoming like God. The gospels show Jesus learning about himself and his goals over time through interactions, in the same ways that humans develop identities. Jesus spends his life and ministry learning how to be himself, frequently asking others and listening to the visions of identity that they provide him. In a sense, in Jesus, God was learning to be human. God was striving to be like us and to learn what it is like to be human. God joined in our own daily struggle to make meaning out of life and to discern who we are in a world where there are no easy answers and maybe no certain, permanent answers ever at all.

Together, we become ourselves. In intimate relationship with God, we discover who we are. We pick up each other's habits, tastes, and patterns of speech, just as any intimate partners do. In learning to live together, we are transformed, each becoming a separate individual, and each becoming like the other. In Jesus, God was physically present as a human. Jesus became human and adult in the same ways that we do—through interaction and transformation, along with vulnerability, uncertainty, and intimacy. As Jesus learns to be like us, we too are developing our own sense of who we are, and we can begin to become ourselves at the same time that we begin to become like Jesus and like the God who has loved us forever.

Living like Jesus

As we live together with Jesus in relationship with God, we become like Jesus and like God. In watching Jesus' embodied ministry, we begin to learn what God does in the world, and before long we begin to share God's values and to become like God in the world. If we are to live in relationship with God, we will become like Jesus in the ways that the gospels portray Jesus as acting.[5]

The story of Jesus' speaking in the synagogue from Isaiah 61 provides one key passage for interpreting how Jesus saw his own work.

> "The Spirit of the Lord is upon me, because he has anointed me to bring good news to the poor. He has sent me to proclaim release to the captives and recovery of sight to the blind, to let the oppressed go free, to proclaim the year of the Lord's favor." (Luke 4:18–19)

This passage offers a number of elements about Jesus' life and

---

[5] For a discussion of how incarnation forms a basis for ministry, see Ronald E. Osborn, *In Christ's Place: Christian Ministry in Today's World* (St. Louis: Bethany Press, 1967), especially 175.

ministry. First is that Jesus is an observant Jew, adherent to the law and faithful in meeting with others for instruction and for the worship of God in community. He had made synagogue attendance his custom. Jesus' relationship with God was not individual; it was something practiced in the community of other believers. It was a custom in that it was something ongoing. A relationship with God is not a once-in-a-lifetime experience, but a continuing habit of living together and getting to know each other. It was that way for Jesus, as well as for other people.

Reading scripture, likewise, was an important practice for Jesus, and in scripture's words he found out about God and about himself. But understanding scripture was not just a habit of devotion or an intellectual endeavor to comprehend an ancient culture. Instead, it was something to be fulfilled in the present. This is not a notion of prophecy, in which ancient words are only words until God performs some action in the present or the future, with an emphasis on the miracle that God knew and communicated beforehand. Instead, the fulfillment of which Jesus speaks is a process of enacting the scripture. He read about God's spirit filling people so that they could announce the year of God's favor, when there would be good news for the poor, the captives, the blind, and the oppressed. To fulfill this scripture means that Jesus joins the ranks of those in all times and places who perform God's tasks. Jesus' practice of reading scripture was to understand better what it means to be God's partner in the present and then to live as fulfillment of that partnership. Such is one of the ways that Jesus became more like God and that Jesus' followers thus become more like God as well.

Jesus' preaching from Isaiah was not an isolated event. It was an opening statement in a conversation with the people there in the synagogue. They reacted strongly to what he had announced, denouncing Jesus and trying to kill him (Luke 4:22–30). The rest of this story shows Jesus' first public speech in a very different light. An embodied ministry is not just announcing God's intentions and working to fulfill them in this world. Partnership with God does not remove one from the realities and difficulties of the world. Instead, we remain in an embodied world that has pains, frustrations, and struggles. In this world, God works mostly at the margins. Jesus performs miracles in Capernaum just as the prophet Elijah saved a widow in Sidon and his successor prophet Elisha healed a man in Syria. God does not try to curry favor in the localities of people who should already be God's partners. Instead, God reaches out to distant lands among mostly unappreciative people—especially after the people from Jesus' hometown of Nazareth try to kill him. God's work is among disbelievers, not among the faithful who are already partners.

Joining with God means accepting this work with the rejected. It means never being at home in the world's comforts, since we have joined with God in the embodied ministry of changing the world. It means seeking the margins of the world, the very places where things can begin to change, where the fabric of a familiar yet wrongly woven world is already starting to unravel. This occurs throughout the stories of Jesus' life and ministry. Jesus speaks the gospel to a frequently married woman at a well in Samaria. He heals the daughter of a Syro-Phoenician woman whom he and many others considered a mere dog. His power goes to a bleeding woman. There is an unpredictability in where Jesus goes and what he does as he moves from one community to another without belonging in any of them. He experiences a homelessness and a rootlessness. He keeps moving, as God's work requires. Partnership with God means moving past this world's attachments to form a family, a life, and a home in God and in the world that we are creating with God, not in the world at hand. From the beginning of Jesus' ministry in that Nazareth synagogue, he is rejected and alone because he has chosen life with God.

There was a purpose to what Jesus did in his life. Jesus formed an identity through interactions with others, and the forming of this identity aligned him with God's purposes, resulting in his rejection by other people. His life on the margins of human existence meant that he lived closer to the new world of God, which is just outside human experience. Jesus often spoke of the purpose of his actions in terms of the Son of man, a term that might also be translated as the human one. In the gospel traditions, the gospel writers frequently used this term to indicate Jesus' own sense of who he was and what he was doing. These statements are infrequent, because the gospels do not portray Jesus' speaking of his work as often as they show things that Jesus taught and did.

One of the most interesting statements of this sort is in a discussion of John the Baptist. Jesus began to express frustration that the people understood neither John nor Jesus, because they were both announcing the reign of God through very different strategies, yet they had some of the same results in that people rejected them both.

> "For John came neither eating nor drinking, and they say, 'He has a demon'; the Son of Man came eating and drinking, and they say, 'Look, a glutton and a drunkard, a friend of tax collectors and sinners!' Yet wisdom is vindicated by her deeds."
> (Matt. 11:18–19)

Jesus came to eat and drink. In simple terms, Jesus came as a human to experience life in very human ways. There is an excessiveness in how Jesus lived life; others felt that he was a glutton and a drunk, and Jesus did not take steps to protect his reputation against these charges. He showed no concern or distress that people thought he ate too much in public or that he drank alcohol, perhaps at times to states of inebriation that would lead others to call him a drunk. Jesus participated fully in life, and no one ever mistook him for a monk or a person of rigid self-control. He acted with joy and energy. Frequently, Jesus is seen at parties, celebrations, and banquets. Although there were times that Jesus withdrew from others for some time alone, he joined in many festive occasions and made friends in a variety of places.

Furthermore, Jesus' companions for these social occasions spanned a large segment of society. He had friends who were drunks and gluttons. He also dined with rabbis, scribes, scholars, and leaders of many sorts. He attended functions with the most respected people of the cities he visited and spent time with governmental collaborators, such as tax collectors. Many of his companions were considered sinners by one segment of society or another. His circle of friends and associates was drawn exceedingly broad. It included wealthy people and the poorest of society; both men and women were present. He spoke with Jews and Gentiles both. In many ways, he refused to draw the distinctions that many other people felt were essential to the maintenance of proper society. Jesus' refusal to live aloof from people echoes in other statements of who he was and what his purpose was to be.

> But Jesus called them to him and said, "You know that the rulers of the Gentiles lord it over them, and their great ones are tyrants over them. It will not be so among you; but whoever wishes to be great among you must be your servant, and

whoever wishes to be first among you must be your slave;
just as the son of man came not to be served but to serve, and
to give his life a ransom for many." (Matt. 20:25–28)

Jesus is not to be a lord. He does not exercise authority over others.
He has no greatness or power that is worthy of respect. Instead, he
sees himself as a slave of others who will serve many.

The path that Jesus takes in the world is not what the world
defines as success. Jesus chooses vulnerability instead of domination.
But it is a path of change, not of protecting the status quo. Rulers and
tyrants look only to their own interests and find their source of privilege in maintaining the ways that things already are. Instead, Jesus
seeks ways to reverse the status quo, to change life from the restricted,
top-down models of the past. Jesus' goal is the radically inclusive life
of God. There is no way to reach that goal of a new world through the
means and strategies of the old world.

Yet the son of man also comes in power. The gospels portray
Jesus as one who takes the form of a slave within the story of his
lifetime, but also as one who will act with great power and authority
within the future. The son of man ushers in apocalyptic times that
change everything in the world (Mark 13:24–33).

Just as Jesus is slave and ransom in order to subvert the status
quo, the apocalyptic visions bring about God's new world. The new
era that Jesus has been announcing will create massive changes. The
coming of God's new world will be both subversive and cataclysmic;
the transition into a radically new way of life will not be easy or direct. In the present, a constant subversion of values and relationships
will work toward the new reality, but at some point, there will be
sudden new alignments that will unsettle and disrupt. Those moments will be like an invasion from another realm, like the clouds
breaking open and letting a new reality dawn upon all.

The opposition between the world and God takes many forms.
The rejection of the prophets, along with contempt and forced suffering, is one part of it. The death of the prophets and the crucifixion
of Jesus are other expressions of the world's resistance to God. The
world does not want to change, because people cling to the advan-
tages that they have gained in the world. God sees a world without
advantage and disadvantage, where the good news of a peaceful realm
can extend to all and where all people can live without fear of each
other. Where humans are addicted to fear, the announcement of God's

reign is a threat because it means withdrawal from that fear and from the ways we protect ourselves against what we fear. When Jesus becomes vulnerable, just as when God becomes flesh, it becomes clear that God's strategy is not about self-protection and about using privilege to keep others away and to prevent harm. Instead, God's strategy for involvement with the world is to begin a world without fear by living without fear, and also without protection, advantage, or privilege. Jesus lives without these things and calls others to join a life where the posturings of this self-protective world begin to look silly instead of necessary and inevitable. The joy that accompanies Jesus' birth becomes a laughter that corrodes the self-importance of people whose lives are invested in the world, and they do not appreciate having their hard-won gains so threatened. They reject Jesus, as they have rejected all God's prophets who announced a very different way of life.

However, the rejection is not life-threatening for Jesus. When the forces of the world wish to take away Jesus' privileges and worldly powers, it is not an issue; he has already given up the systems of privilege. Jesus strives to reach those who have been rejected, for they must be the first to learn this new way of life. The realm of God becomes a place of vulnerability without fear; the people who are rejected by the world are already halfway there because they have learned to live with their vulnerability, whereas the powerful cling to both the illusion of self-protection and the driving fear that propels their systems of privilege.

Jesus came to seek the lost (Luke 15:4–32; 19:10). Jesus came to work among the rejected, the vulnerable, the disadvantaged, and the marginalized. The initial announcement of his ministry was to bring good news to the poor, the captives, the blind, and the oppressed (Luke 4:18). Throughout his ministry, Jesus reached out to children, to elderly persons, to women, to foreign persons such as Samaritans and Syro-Phoenicians, to those who had damaged bodies or deep illnesses, to those possessed with evil and impurity, and to those who lived as tax collectors, prostitutes, political radicals, and others. These and so many like them are the first residents of God's new world. Rich and powerful persons from ruling classes may join them, for they too are lost. Jesus strives to create an inclusive world by bringing together those who have been rejected and ending their exclusion.

Living for God

Living with Jesus means learning about ourselves and about God at the same time. There is a synergy involved in the interpersonal dynamics; we become ourselves as God takes on human form. We and God together learn to share a common mission in the world as we experience together what it means to be human and what it means to announce the reign of God within the world as it is.

Life with Jesus leads us to a commitment to God's cause and an involvement in bringing this vision to reality. With God, we are intimately concerned about the world that we love. We are invested and involved in bringing this world into God's reign. This is a high-risk enterprise, and it is bound to be full of frustrations and disappointments as we too experience the world's rejection. God's goals of inclusion, healing, reversal, subversion, fearlessness, celebration, and love become our goals, and we face the same resistance that Jesus did. Our love for God causes us to entwine our lives, and so our futures are bound up in one another. We are known for the same tasks and missions, and the process of transforming the world is shared within this love. In Jesus, we have learned what it will mean for us to bring this vision of God's reign into reality. We will experience rejection as we seek the lost. We will be excluded as we seek to include. We will live our lives as wanderers, never at home in this world because we have transferred our citizenship to the realm of God, even though our work here has only just begun.

In the incarnation, we learn of God, and God learns of us. There is a depth to the knowledge of each other that we forge in Jesus and that we continue to build as we work together for God's purposes. The work that we need to do together was seen clearly in Jesus' life. After watching Jesus, we cannot claim that we do not know how to live in God's new world. Likewise, we must admit that we know exactly what the cost will be. The love for God that empowers this relationship is not something that the world will accept easily. The more deeply we express this love and the more that we implement God's plans for human life, the more opposition we will find. In Jesus, we have heard the announcement of God's reign; we have seen God's plans begin to take form; we have learned how to embrace more nearly the God whom we love; and we have experienced the utter joy of life together with God. But we have also known loss, for Jesus' life faces the brutality of the world's reaction against the one whom we love.

7

WHY JESUS DIED

Explanations for God's presence in Jesus' life have challenged the church for two thousand years. The desire to know God has often ended up as a drive to understand God and Jesus, to define and explain them so that the whole story makes perfect sense. But God's ways are not ours, and God's presence remains unpredictable, so we can never quite explain what God was doing and why it all happened the way it did. Even if Jesus' life makes sense, his death is even harder to understand. After a few years of Jesus' ministry of announcing God's desire for people, government officials executed him as a criminal. Understanding why Jesus died is full of potential problems. Did God abandon Jesus to death? Did God plan for Jesus to die, taking the role of conspirator in this murder? Was Jesus' death a surprise to God? Or was God unable to prevent Jesus' death? And how can we explain the testimony of several followers that Jesus' tomb was found empty and that they saw Jesus alive in the flesh weeks after his death?

Concerning Jesus' life, the gospels are clear that Jesus was human, embodied, and enfleshed. He ate and drank like human bodies do; he grew and aged like people do; he slept and awoke like all flesh.

The gospels never seriously question Jesus' humanity; he lived in the same way that humans always live. Because Jesus is human, it was inevitable that he would die, even if the gospels never state it so bluntly and even if so much of the church's tradition has avoided this realization. Those who are born will die.

The implications for any understanding of incarnation are immense. If God is embodied in Jesus, this embodied God will die. Whatever is established in Jesus will end in death. This is how human life works; it begins in birth and ends in death. For humans, there is no forever on this earth. There is only the span of time from now until death. For God to become human, to take on human flesh, means that this body of God will die.

To be sure, there are ways around this problem—at least, God has options for how to escape death. Many theologies have depended on God's ability to escape death, either by leaving Jesus' body at the last minute so that it is not God who dies on the cross, or by the death itself's being less real because it is only temporary. Some have seen humanity as almost a costume that God puts on and then takes off just as it begins to be too distressing to play the part of human any longer.

But these options seem to ring hollow when one reads the gospels. In the stories of Jesus, there is no clear understanding that Jesus should have been immortal. All those around Jesus saw his humanity and experienced daily life with him as a human. Never did anyone comment that Jesus would not die. Certainly, the disciples were not eager to think of Jesus' death. When Jesus discusses his impending death with his disciples, they argue with him and he rebukes them (Mark 8:31–33), but never does it seem that anyone expects that Jesus will never die. They argue only about the timing and cause. The gospels present no reason to think that Jesus would not die by natural causes, if only he lived long enough.

God's decision to be physically present with humans in the world through Jesus is a decision to be invested in human life. This means its joys and sorrows, its pains and delights, and also its death. Human life is bound up in time, and the time for life ends.

Of course, what happened with Jesus is far more distressing than this. His death was not the natural end to a full and long life. It was not a peaceful slipping away from earthly existence as the body completes its aging. Instead, it was a brutal murder, a state-sponsored execution in the prime of life. Other humans, people like us, took their hands and used tools of death to end Jesus' life. Our human abandonment of God's vision for the world, our human rejection of God's partnership with Jesus and with us to transform all creation into the reign of God, and our human resistance to God's intention combined in an act of execution when Jesus died.

But the story does not end there. Christian tradition asserts that God raised Jesus from death. Flesh once dead lived again.

The Bible is strangely uninterested in explaining how these events happened. In ancient Greek thought, it was certainly possible for gods to be killed. Furthermore, Jesus is not the only resurrection recorded in the New Testament. Just as Elijah raised a woman's son from death (1 Kgs. 17:17–24), Jesus raised a widow's son from death (Luke 7:11–17) and resurrected Lazarus (John 11), and even Paul was able to bring back a person from the dead (Acts 20:7–12).

There are no explanations for resurrection. No one in the Bible claims to know how it happens or what it means in physical terms. There is no speculation about whether Jesus' body is the same body he had before or whether it is a different body. Jesus eats after his death and resurrection; he touches things and is touched; and yet he is hard to recognize and can disappear easily (although suddenly getting lost in a crowd is a skill that Jesus possessed from his earlier days).

The New Testament never makes a point of the physics of the resurrection. It can even be said that the New Testament is not very interested in the theology of the resurrection. Instead, the biblical texts focus more on the presence and relationship involved: Jesus is once more present to his disciples and followers.

Why Some People Think Jesus Died

Since Jesus died, people have been trying to understand the event and its meaning. There is a seemingly infinite diversity of options for interpreting the death of Jesus, but two general approaches characterize a large number of the theories that have been developed. One approach is the notion of sacrificial atonement, and the other is the idea of moral persuasion.[1]

---

[1]For examples of the standard theological approaches, see Daniel L. Migliore, *Faith Seeking Understanding: An Introduction to Christian Theology* (Grand Rapids: Eerdmans, 1991), 151–61; and Clark M. Williamson, *Way of Blessing, Way of Life: A Christian Theology* (St. Louis: Chalice Press, 1999), 210–21.

Sacrificial atonement theories argue that Jesus died as a sacrifice to atone for the sins of human beings. To understand the meaning of Jesus' death according to these theories, we must first set the death within a larger context of God's activity in the world. God created humanity to live in harmony with God and with all of creation. However, humans began to sin, violating the order that God intended and destroying the harmony. Although God continued to love humans, God could not abide sin and disobedience.

As a result, human sin has angered God. The alienation between them must be healed, and right relationship must be restored, but because sin is disobedience, it requires punishment. God cannot let sin go unpunished, and the penalty is death. But killing the people will not restore the relationship or enable obedience. So God comes to earth as Jesus, the only sinless human there has ever been. Because he is human, he can die, but because he has never sinned, he is not under the death penalty. Jesus volunteers to sacrifice himself for the rest of us. God enforces the death penalty against an innocent party, thus fulfilling the necessary punishment. But because God has not killed us, the relationship can be restored, as long as humans remain obedient and avoid sin. Jesus has paid the price.

This view is the most established and widely accepted option in the history of the church's tradition. It certainly has roots in the New Testament, at least in certain interpretations of Paul. Paul refers to Jesus as the one "whom God put forward as a sacrifice of atonement" (Rom. 3:25).[2] Other traditions emphasize Jesus' death as *self-sacrifice*. But even if Jesus volunteered for death, the idea of sacrifice still requires a God who desires this kind of sacrifice and who chooses death for people who have sinned. God is still portrayed as a God of wrath, consumed by anger and unable to stop without lashing out and killing, even though God can be distracted by killing an innocent instead of killing the guilty. If Jesus chose this role for himself, it was in accord with God's desire. In the theology of sacrificial atonement, relationship with God means obedience, which means death at God's own hand.

The theory of sacrificial atonement has several difficulties. It shows a God who desires death. God knew that exterminating humanity

---

[2]Note, however, that the passage continues and describes the purpose of the crucifixion as proof of Jesus' righteousness. Cf. Romans 5:8–9.

was a possibility, and yet God chose to set up the rules that way from the start. The theory of sacrificial atonement presents a bloodthirsty God, and the good news of the gospel and the incarnation becomes the news that God is willing to murder and sacrifice God's own beloved child.[3]

If Jesus' sacrifice was voluntary, the theory presents us with a suicidal savior who may encourage others in similar self-destruction.[4]

Many Christians have felt that atonement theories introduce more problems than they solve, so other explanations have grown alongside them. The idea of moral persuasion has a long and distinguished history. This explanation holds that God became human in Jesus Christ in order to persuade humans that obedience to God's will is possible and desirable. Jesus becomes a primary example for humans to follow because Jesus proves that it is possible to live a sinless and pure human life in the face of great opposition. Jesus even endured the suffering of the cross and remained faithful. Whatever the rest of us face in life, we can draw hope from the fact that Jesus suffered more and stayed faithful through it.

In this interpretation, Jesus becomes very much like other martyrs of the faith throughout history. These role models encourage present believers to remain faithful to God no matter what the circumstances.

Moral persuasion approaches can emphasize God's love, especially in contrast to the sacrificial theories' tendency to portray God's wrath. God loved the world so much that God chose incarnation even though it would mean opposition and death. Although this explanation still makes death the ultimate proof of love, it does emphasize God's deep commitment to relationship with humanity as the basis for everything that happens in Jesus' life and death.

---

[3]Many of the difficulties stem from Christian interpreters' own unfamiliarity with the sacrificial systems of ancient Israel and of the Greco-Roman world of the New Testament, which provide the grounding for the metaphors of sacrifice. See Jon L. Berquist, "What Does the Lord Require? Old Testament Child Sacrifice and New Testament Christology," *Encounter* 55/2 (April 1994): 107–28.

[4]In particular, this theology has victimized women. See Joanne Carlson Brown and Carole R. Bohn, eds., *Christianity, Patriarchy, and Abuse: A Feminist Critique* (New York: Pilgrim Press, 1989). See also Rita Nakashima Brock's work in relation to such christological problems in *Journeys by Heart: A Christology of Erotic Power* (New York: Crossroad, 1988). A helpful discussion can be found in L. Susan Bond, *Trouble with Jesus: Women, Christology, and Preaching* (St. Louis: Chalice Press, 1999), especially her idea of the "Icon of the Battered Woman," 30–32.

Although these theories make helpful attempts to explain the crucifixion of Jesus, they all are incomplete. They do better at interpreting the later New Testament's reflections on the crucifixion than they do at echoing the gospels' own accounts of why Jesus died. They may emphasize obedience and God's love, but they run the risk of losing the context, not only of Jesus' life, but of all the ways that God has been present with us. Moreover, these theories demand a high price for adherence. All these approaches place too much emphasis on the value of Jesus' forced and untimely death. There are dangers if we idealize or idolize this murderous act of crucifixion. To avoid these dangers, we must work to develop explanations that make sense in terms of the gospel narratives.[5]

The Cross in the New Testament

Perhaps the most striking element of the New Testament's interpretation of Jesus' crucifixion is the inevitability of it all. Repeatedly the gospels assert that Jesus had to die; there were no other alternatives and no other way for the story of Jesus to end. From the proclamations in each gospel that Jesus must suffer and die in Jerusalem to the hints in some that all the events were scripted in prior prophecy, the gospels understand that the death of Jesus had to take place.

Jesus' death was inevitable because Jesus was human, and all humans die. If Jesus was going to face every human experience, he would need to face death. If he did not die, he was not human. Incarnation makes death inevitable, just as every birth is inevitably followed by death—although that birth does not determine the circumstances or timing of that death.

Also, human opposition to Jesus seems inevitable. His commitment to God's agenda for human life makes many enemies for Jesus, including enemies in powerful positions. In retrospect, one could have known that this would happen were God to come to earth. Inevitably, at least some people would want to kill God and any of God's emissaries, as they had prophets and numerous others who followed God.

This is are the gospels' understanding of Jesus' death. Because Jesus was alive and was human, his death was natural and inevitable.

---

[5]For a thorough treatment of the New Testament passages related to resurrection of Jesus and others, see Richard N. Longenecker, ed., *Life in the Face of Death: The Resurrection Message of the New Testament* (Grand Rapids: Eerdmans, 1998).

It was an inevitable result of the fact that Jesus was alive and that all living things die as part of living. That his death was a murder, albeit a state-sanctioned execution, was an inevitable result of the way that Jesus lived because his commitment to God angered those who resisted God. From these shared assumptions, the gospels each develop different interpretations of Jesus' death.

Matthew

Perhaps more than any other gospel, the gospel of Matthew represents the ideas about Jesus' crucifixion and resurrection that have become most popular throughout Christianity.

When Jesus is born, Matthew interprets it as a political act that draws the attention of foreign sages and local kings alike, and that leads to changes in policy, including the massacre of young boys to prevent Jesus from rising up as a political threat to King Herod (Matt. 2:1–18). Later, as soon as the disciples begin to recognize that Jesus is the Messiah and is the Son of God (Matt. 16:13–20), Jesus makes the first of his announcements that it is necessary for him to be killed so that he might rise again (Matt. 16:21–24; see also 17:22–23 and 20:17–19). The leaders soon begin their plotting to kill Jesus.

Matthew's gospel narrates the events leading to the crucifixion, including a trial and sentencing. The government executed Jesus as a state criminal, but at his death, the Roman guard and others nearby realized that Jesus was the Son of God (Matt. 27:54). One of Jesus' followers, a man named Joseph, placed Jesus in a tomb and set a large rock in front of it while Mary and Mary Magdalene were watching (Matt. 27:57–61). As soon as Jesus was in the tomb, the leaders realized that they were at risk; if the body were stolen, Jesus' followers could claim that he had been brought back to life, and the leaders' political position would once more be threatened by such a rumor (Matt. 27:62–66). Thus, they set a guard to watch the tomb and to secure it against such theft.

When Mary and Mary Magdalene went the next day to see the tomb, an angel appeared and rolled the stone away. This frightened the guards and the women, but the angel comforted them and told them that Jesus was not in the tomb.

> But the angel said to the women, "Do not be afraid; I know that you are looking for Jesus who was crucified. He is not here; for he has been raised, as he said. Come, see the place

where he lay. Then go quickly and tell his disciples, 'He has been raised from the dead, and indeed he is going ahead of you to Galilee; there you will see him.'" (Matt. 28:5–7)

As the women hurried to tell others, filled with a mixture of fear and joy, they saw Jesus, who repeated the angel's claim that Jesus was on his way to Galilee. Meanwhile, the guards also left, and they returned to the leaders, who decided to say publicly that the tomb had been raided (Matt. 28:11–15).

In Galilee, the disciples (now eleven after Judas' suicide) gathered at a mountain. Jesus then appeared to them. Seeing him, some of them worshiped; others disbelieved. Jesus then pronounced the gospel's final words:

And Jesus came and said to them, "All authority in heaven and on earth has been given to me. Go therefore and make disciples of all nations, baptizing them in the name of the Father and of the Son and of the Holy Spirit, and teaching them to obey everything that I have commanded you. And remember, I am with you always, to the end of the age." (Matt. 28:18–20)

With this, the gospel of Matthew comes to a close. Amazingly, there is no explanation of how the resurrection happened, let alone why it did. It is not clear if the disciples ever saw Jesus again or what Jesus did afterward. The reader does not begin to know what Jesus looked like. Instead, the story ends with his crucifixion and resurrection and with a final command to the disciples that they go.

This version of the story presents the core elements that have remained at the center of the church's proclamation ever since. Although the gospel itself never describes the actual resurrection, it tells about its aftermath. Jesus was alive and talked to people, at least a few of them. Jesus remained present with them, but there is no indication that Jesus' physical, bodily presence continued for very long after the crucifixion. They do not preach Jesus' resurrection as the core of their faith. Instead, they are commanded to repeat Jesus' teaching and to live in the sense of Jesus' presence.

The result of Jesus' crucifixion, therefore, is that Jesus' message spreads, through the disciples, even farther than before. These same disciples who had been sent all throughout the territory near to Jesus' ministry (Matt. 10) are now sent to the ends of the earth with the same message of Jesus' teachings. Crucifixion unleashes Jesus' power to travel more widely than ever before.

Mark

In contrast, Mark tells a shorter, simpler, and starker story.[6] In Mark, Joseph buries Jesus' body, but the body is not watched by soldiers, and there is no concern on the part of the politicians to make sure that rumors of Jesus' being alive are discounted. The two Marys are joined by Salome in their visit to the tomb, where they find a young man dressed in white who tells them this:

> But he said to them, "Do not be alarmed; you are looking for Jesus of Nazareth, who was crucified. He has been raised; he is not here. Look, there is the place they laid him. But go, tell his disciples and Peter that he is going ahead of you to Galilee; there you will see him, just as he told you." (Mark 16:6–7)

As a result, they flee from the tomb in fear and do not say anything to anyone (Mark 16:8). This is a sudden ending to the book, and it leaves far too many issues unanswered to comfort most readers. Many ancient sources added various endings to the book. Some of those endings are much like Matthew's version of accounts and may well have been written by people who had read Matthew, Luke, or some other similar gospel. Other endings differ considerably from anything else in the gospels and seem to reflect some very different ideas of the early church and its beliefs about Jesus. However, the version of the gospel that ends at Mark 16:8 is the most reliably accurate version of the gospel story that exists in ancient manuscripts, and it is probably the way that the author wrote the story.

The ending is quite shocking to modern Christian readers. Jesus has no appearances at all after the resurrection. The women who see Jesus do not see an angel (only a "young man"), do not see Jesus, and do not tell their story to anyone else. Although the young man promises that they will see Jesus in Galilee, the appearance is not recorded. As a result, Jesus has no final words. The last that anyone saw Jesus, he was dead. The modern reader assumes that Jesus is alive, and so that the young man's speech refers to a living Jesus instead of a corpse.

---

[6]Many scholars believe that Mark's gospel was written before the other three canonical gospels, based mostly on the principle that the story of Jesus' life and death probably began as a shorter, relatively unadorned story, and then grew into something more complex.

But this is only an assumption. The young man never quite claims that Jesus is alive. Instead, he says things that make perfectly good sense no matter whether Jesus is dead or alive, and he never tells them which one is the case.

The gospel of Mark, then, ends with a very strange and disturbing conclusion. The reader cannot know what happened to Jesus from just reading this gospel. It ends in a mystery. But somehow, for this gospel, that is enough. The statement of faith has already been made: The Roman soldier proclaimed that Jesus is the Son of God. Jesus' teachings have all been proclaimed, and his miracles have been witnessed by the crowds. Those who have heard Jesus have had the opportunity to make up their own minds whether to believe or to reject him. In the end, the teachings are all that matters—and the fact that the tomb is empty. Wherever Jesus is and whether he is alive or dead, a different question lingers for the readers. Will we follow Jesus' teachings or not, and will we believe that Jesus is the Son of God, the embodiment of what God wishes to have done in the world? Those are the important questions. The gospel of Mark does not emphasize what happened to Jesus after his death. Instead, the only important thing is what other people do, and ultimately what we do, after Jesus' crucifixion.

Luke

The gospel of Luke offers a very different strategy to telling the story of Jesus' crucifixion and what came next.

In Luke, the Roman guard at the foot of the cross merely proclaims Jesus innocent, rather than calling him the Son of God (Luke 23:47). Luke makes it clear that the women who had been at the foot of the cross watched everything while Joseph buried Jesus. Many people see the empty tomb, and two men state that Jesus has been raised from the dead (Luke 24:5–7). But Jesus does not appear nearby. When Jesus appears (Luke 24), he does so three times: on the road to Emmaus, to the eleven disciples, and then to a group who witness Jesus' leaving the earth and ascending to heaven. But Luke continues his story in the book of Acts, which tells of how God's spirit empowers the church to announce the same vision of God that Jesus did.

Thus, for Luke in the books of Luke and Acts, the gospel story is not the story of Jesus. It is the story of how God is transforming the world, starting in Nazareth, proceeding to Jerusalem, and continuing to Rome and the entire empire. At each step, God's message as carried by the Holy Spirit faces opposition and rejection, and the messengers are persecuted and sometimes killed. Jesus was the first to preach this message, echoing God's prophets of former days, and so Jesus was the first to be killed—but not the last one to preach or to be executed for preaching this transforming message of God's new world.

Neither Jesus' crucifixion nor his resurrection is the climax of the gospel of Luke-Acts. Both of them are transitions to the coming of the Holy Spirit upon the disciples. Previously, God's spirit had resided within Jesus, but the reader of the gospel already knows that Jesus' true ministry is to give the Holy Spirit to others (Luke 3:16).

Luke thus presents an altogether different way to envision the events of Jesus' life. For this gospel, God's work begins in ancient times with prophets and continues in the life of the church as it proclaims the message that transforms the world through the power of the Spirit. By living and dying as he did, Jesus enabled all to have this Holy Spirit.

John

The gospel of John is quite different from the other three canonical gospels. Joseph buried Jesus with the help of Nicodemus (John 19:38–42). After the disciples discovered that the tomb was empty, Mary Magdalene stayed by the tomb, crying. Two angels appeared to her to ask her why she was crying. When she explained that Jesus had been taken away, she turned around and saw Jesus. But she did not recognize him, because Jesus looked different. In response, Jesus told her not to touch him.

In the next scenes, Jesus appeared to the disciples by walking through a locked door, and he breathed the Holy Spirit onto them (John 20:22–23). Although Jesus appears again, this is the climactic point of John's gospel. Jesus was the one sent by God to baptize with the Holy Spirit (John 1:33), and Jesus performed this baptism as soon as he gathered with the disciples after his resurrection (John 20:19–23).

Jesus' passing from the world means that the Spirit of God will live with us directly and forever. This is the spirit that Jesus breathes onto the disciples (John 20:22), and the spirit has lived on in Jesus' followers ever since.

Paul

At the same time that the gospels were being written and the traditions about Jesus were being passed around orally among the early Christians, other interpreters and leaders of the faith were speaking and writing to the churches that were forming throughout the Roman Empire. More of Paul's writings survive than those of any other early leaders. In one of his considerations of the cross, Paul describes the crucifixion and resurrection as foolishness.

> For the message about the cross is foolishness to those who are perishing, but to us who are being saved it is the power of God.
>
> ....
>
> We proclaim Christ crucified, a stumbling block to Jews and foolishness to Gentiles, but to those who are the called, both Jews and Greeks, Christ the power of God and the wisdom of God. (1 Cor. 1:18, 23–24)

In the crucifixion of Jesus, Paul sees utter folly. The cross shows how God refuses both philosophy and power to establish something that is stronger than either: the bonds of life together. In Christ, God shared what was common with humanity, even death. God embraced the parts of our existence that we think of as failures, even dying a death of state execution.

The cross, for Paul, is a place of commonality. In a divided culture and a fragmented church, the cross shattered divisions (Eph. 2:12–16). In death, Jesus experiences something common to all groups. No social class or racial group escapes death; it is something we all face. Jesus' death brings God into contact with what we all hold in common, rather than our relationship with God being based on any special privilege that one group might have over another. The cross becomes the place where God and humanity are united, and thus where all humanity is reconciled with each other.

This commonality is also a source of continuing life. What Jesus experienced in death and resurrection is not something that is for Jesus alone because in the events of Jesus' life, God forged a bond of relationship with us. In Christ, we all die and are raised to eternal life. Christ is something we all share; Christ brings us together as one group (Rom. 6:3–14). The transformation of death into the new life of God changes us all completely. The old state of being ends, and we become parts of God's new world. We are alive to God; we do not live under any human jurisdiction nor under the laws of any other way of life. We are God's. Our relationship with God is all that matters and the only thing that shapes our individual and communal lives.

All the rules have changed; we live by God's grace. That is, we live because God has decided that we will live and desires us to live with God. Nothing, not even death, stands in the way of this unbounded intimacy with God. In this way, Paul can write of the cross as a point for starting anew in life. Because it is death to the world and the sign of an unstoppable relationship with God, the cross points to the newness of this life of intimacy (Gal. 5:22–26; 6:14–15).

Thus, for Paul, the cross as the symbol of Jesus' death and resurrection means many things. Paul typically focuses on the cross as the place of Jesus' death, wherein God takes on the fullness of human life so as to ground the relationship with humanity in that which humans hold most common. In Jesus' death, God comes closer to us than ever before.

Why Jesus Died

As the early church struggled to understand what Jesus' life, death, and resurrection meant to them and to the faith, they developed a range of options. Over many years, some of these options received sufficient acceptance that they became part of the canon of the New Testament. All of the canonical interpretations emphasized that Jesus was human and that his death was real. There was a death; there was a corpse; and the inability to locate that corpse three days later did not change those facts. After those agreements, the consensus does not continue. Instead, the early church produced a variety of understandings and embraced them all, leaving for believers today a legacy that accepted diverse ways of interpreting Jesus' death and resurrection.

Mark's gospel portrays how Jesus lives on in memory, as well as in the community of believers, who may well be overwhelmed by fear but manage to speak to each other. Matthew's story is a story of gospel, of how the good news began and how it began to be spread when the disciples who had devoted their lives to Jesus did not stay near the risen Christ to worship him. Instead, they went away. Both Matthew and Mark echo the words of the prophet Zechariah: "Strike the shepherd, that the sheep may be scattered" (Zech. 13:7; cf. Matt.

26:31 and Mark 14:27). When Jesus is crucified, Jesus' followers disperse into the world. The effect of Jesus' death by crucifixion, as well as of whatever happens afterward, is for the disciples to go into the world. Jesus' death takes away any center from the believers, and the gospel spreads.

For Luke, the key figure is not Jesus, but the spirit of God that empowers God's work as manifest both in Jesus and in the church. The death and resurrection of Jesus only point to what God will do in the life of the church. Likewise, the gospel of John understands Jesus' death as no more than a temporary setback, because death could not be permanent for a spiritual being such as Jesus. Jesus returns from death in an even more spiritual form, untouchable but still capable of imparting spirit to others.

Paul's writings understand the death and resurrection of Jesus as foolishness and a stumbling block; it is hard to believe how and why the leader of faith died. Yet in that death, we find God experiencing the common experience of all humanity. From that point on, everything is different. God makes all things new.

Why Jesus Lives

Yet, if the death of Jesus challenges theology to explain something difficult, so does Jesus' resurrection life. Here the gospels find even less on which to agree. This should not be surprising; human life gives us many examples of death, but our common experience gives us no way to understand one raised from the dead. Mark seems not to know of Jesus' resurrection, or at least Mark refuses to make clear reference to Jesus, whom no one sees alive at the end of the gospel. Matthew sees Jesus as ascending; John thinks of an untouchable Jesus in a different kind of body. Luke and John both see Jesus as present only for little more than whatever time it takes to impart the Spirit to his followers. Paul makes an interesting argument, assuming that Jesus' death and his resurrection both reflect the common human experiences—and therefore the resurrection will come for all people. Just because we see Jesus as the first resurrected person does not mean that Jesus is the only one; it only means that Jesus is first, and it is reasonable to assume that all people after their deaths will be raised to life again by God. Jesus is not unique, only early.

In all the New Testament, there is surprisingly little emphasis on the miracle of resurrection. Theologies that consider the resurrection as a miraculous event of cosmic power and earth-shattering import thus become difficult to defend as interpretations of scripture.

The New Testament insists that resurrection is the ground for a new kind of relationship with God, a partnership that now knows no limits, not even the limit of death. God's persistent desire for humanity outlives even death. God's love is unstoppable. God gains nothing through Jesus' death; there is no magical substitution or atonement that settles the divine accounts and frees God to love us on the other side of a punishing death. Instead, the New Testament presents an image of God who moves consistently to restore and provide life, especially through the spirit and the church that are God's loving gifts to the whole world. The death of Jesus does not save us, but God moves in all circumstances, even death, to bring life.[7] We see those moves most clearly when God's desire for life is contrasted with the human murder of God's incarnation in Jesus.

However, the contrast remains. In Jesus, people found God to be present more intimately than ever before. God's physical presence took human form and for a while lived among us. But when Jesus died, there was absence. In Mark, the absence of God and Jesus is striking, as most disciples are scattered and the remaining faithful women are filled with terror at the sight of the empty tomb. But the other gospels face this stark absence as well; whether Jesus ascends into heaven or not, there comes a day when no one sees Jesus ever again. The chance to see God in human form passes away from human experience, at least until the end of time in scenes like those from the conclusion to the book of Revelation. Jesus is gone; whether dead from crucifixion or alive in resurrection, Jesus is gone. The spirit and the church are all that are left. Resurrected, brought back to life to live among us once more, Jesus leaves. His followers scatter or else huddle together in abandonment. Like lovers abandoned and dejected, facing an aloneness that rips their souls, they know that Jesus is gone.

The resurrection leaves only a trace of Jesus as it leaves a hole in the center of the faith. The early church kept echoing this emptiness. God does not stay with us; God does not even leave a body for us to see and touch; God grants us no place to serve as shrine and center of memory. With nothing at our core but the absence of Jesus and the

---

[7]The notion that resurrection shows the unstoppability of God is frequent in theology. See, for instance, Clark M. Williamson, *Way of Blessing, Way of Life: A Christian Theology* (St. Louis: Chalice Press, 1999), 200–202.

memory-trace of where God was once incarnate, our faith is allowed no center. Nothing brings us together, as Matthew recognizes when he ends the gospel with Jesus' sending the disciples to the corners of the earth. The followers of Jesus are those who leave, who abandon their families, who worship at no sanctuary but only in spirit, who have no place to lay their heads, who have no family to call their own, who wander to the ends of the earth with the message of this God who came and left.

The faith of these followers remains uncentered. The emptiness of the tomb becomes an emptiness at our core, and we can never afford any attempt to place something besides a vacant grave as the foundation for faith. We cannot turn our attention inward, nor can we look only at the past. With the women on Easter morning, we face the emptiness and flee, and our terror drives us out into the world, where the message of God in Jesus echoes in our own words as we announce God's desires to the whole world. No shrine pulls us together. No structure or organization binds us together as an institution. No mountaintop of transfiguration may dare become the place where we remember Jesus. Nothing must ever take Jesus' place at our center, even if that place is as vacant as an empty tomb. In fear we run, for the shepherd has been struck and we, like sheep, scatter. We are scattered like seed, and therein lies hope for a growth that can transform the world.

8

THE BODY OF CHRIST

If Jesus is the incarnation of God, then after the events of the gospels, God's incarnation is over. The gospels record the last appearance of Jesus in flesh differently: in Mark, while Jesus was yet a corpse; in Matthew and Luke, at the ascension after many appearances by Jesus; in John, over a breakfast discussion with the disciples. However, all of them portray a Jesus who was seen and touched, but now no longer. Jesus' body has disappeared forever, or at least until the end of time at the conclusion of the book of Revelation. Jesus' fleshly life on earth had a beginning and an end; the crucifixion, the resurrection, and the ascension of Jesus mark the cessation of his physical presence among humans. God's days in flesh have ended.

What happens next?

The Old Testament depicted a God who was frequently present with God's people in embodied form. The New Testament tells no more such stories throughout the rest of its pages until the very end of the book of Revelation when Christ appears in the new heaven and the new earth to host a banquet in the new Jerusalem. In the streets of our world, the earth that we now inhabit, Jesus' feet never walk again.

No one sees God in the flesh again.[1] Jesus is the last appearance of God, and the resurrection is the disappearance of God.

Certainly, the experience of God lingers, as does the memory of God. The coming of the spirit allows the presence of God to be felt, even when God is not seen and cannot be touched again. The spirit empowers believers in the New Testament and afterward to form partnership with God by embracing the goals and purposes that Jesus proclaimed and that had always been close to God's heart. But after the strikingly embodied, incarnate presence of God in Jesus, the spirit can seem but a trace of God's presence, a mark of where God used to be, a hearkening back to the days when God was with us in flesh.

God's body in the world ceased to appear directly in Old Testament times, and in the New Testament, God's incarnation in Jesus also disappeared. What presence does God still have in the world? This question echoes and lingers, always remaining after the gospels. The theological assertions about God's incarnation in Jesus are more than statements about God's past activity. To claim that God was present in Jesus, who lived, died, and was raised from the dead, is to make a theological assertion wrapped in history. It is a statement about the past, focusing on what God did two thousand years ago. But the idea of incarnation is also a statement about God's character and about the kind of activity in which God continues to engage in the world. Incarnation insists that the God whom we love is not a God who was present, but a God who is present, incarnate, embodied—even though the body has disappeared.

The early church struggled with this problem. This chapter investigates in particular how Paul developed a way that the church should understand God's physical presence in the world. How does a faith in history, based in a story of what happened in the past, become a present faith? We tell the story that God once walked among us in visible, embodied flesh, but no longer. Perhaps this is why the gospels focus so much on retracing the life of Jesus, and why the New Testament canon begins with the gospels' fourfold repetition of the story. It is like retracing steps over and over, searching for the point

---

[1]Paul, in his conversion, hears the voice of Jesus and sees a blinding light (Acts 9:4–6). He does not see Jesus; in fact, the event leaves him incapable of any vision for a time. Paul later has mystical visions, as does John in the book of Revelation, but these are not experiences of Jesus as God in human flesh in this world.

where a loved one was lost. In obsession, we revisit the life of Jesus and look for the exact moment when God left, wondering if perhaps we can understand where God went, since we no longer see God with us. God as Immanuel, God with us, has become God invisible. Where do we find God? The search begins with retracing the steps where we last saw God. How does belief occur in the absence of God's body, or is God present in some other way?

Does God have any body left in the world?

The Body of God

The gospels fixate upon the body of Jesus, in life and in death. This body, God in human flesh, was killed on a cross and placed in a tomb. Three days later—during which time the tomb was unwatched, at least for a time—the body of Jesus disappeared. In Mark, the body is never seen again, whereas in the other gospels, God raises Jesus from the dead and the body of Jesus walks the earth again. In Matthew and Luke, Jesus' resurrected bodily life on earth continues until the ascension, after which Jesus is not on earth again. For John, Jesus is never touchable, not quite physical, and is never seen to go away permanently. In these interpretations of God's incarnation in Jesus, the death and resurrection are marks of God's absence; they represent God going away and leaving us alone. The aloneness is starkest in Mark, and at the end of the gospel there is fear at the prospect of living life alone. In Luke and John, the spirit comes as comfort; in Matthew, Jesus gives the disciples a mission and leaves them alone with their work.

Paul takes this aloneness as the beginning point for his own theological reflection. He preaches Christ crucified. The execution of God's Messiah, of God incarnate, is the cornerstone of faith, where paradoxically it all begins to make sense. Paul rejects the notions of wisdom and deep philosophical explanations. Paul is not concerned with rational reasons why to believe.[2] Instead, Paul points to the emotions of fear and weakness. This is where faith begins. The essence of the cross, the most important thing about Jesus, is the fear that we feel at the absence of God.

---

[2]One must be careful when reading Paul's rhetoric. He claims that he is presenting a plain, unadorned argument, and yet his writings are full of rhetorical devices—including the claim that he is not using rhetoric.

When I came to you, brothers and sisters, I did not come proclaiming the mystery of God to you in lofty words or wisdom. For I decided to know nothing among you except Jesus Christ, and him crucified. And I came to you in weakness and in fear and in much trembling. My speech and my proclamation were not with plausible words of wisdom, but with a demonstration of the Spirit and of power, so that your faith might rest not on human wisdom but on the power of God. (1 Cor. 2:1–5)

Paul claims to know nothing. If there is to be any foundation at all for Paul's belief, it will be Jesus—and not the Jesus of Easter faith, but the Jesus of Good Friday, crucified on a cross and sealed in a tomb. The idea of Christ as cornerstone is echoed elsewhere.

So then you are no longer strangers and aliens, but you are citizens with the saints and also members of the household of God, built upon the foundation of the apostles and prophets, with Christ Jesus himself as the cornerstone. In him the whole structure is joined together and grows into a holy temple in the Lord; in whom you also are built together spiritually into a dwelling place for God. (Eph. 2:19–22)

The image develops here explicitly as a temple, a building based on the foundation of the apostles and prophets arranged around the cornerstone of Jesus. Together, all believers make up a temple in which God dwells. We are the stones that form the building. A later New Testament writer expands upon this theme and connects it back to Old Testament texts.

Come to him, a living stone, though rejected by mortals yet chosen and precious in God's sight, and like living stones, let yourselves be built into a spiritual house, to be a holy priesthood, to offer spiritual sacrifices acceptable to God through Jesus Christ. For it stands in scripture:

"See, I am laying in Zion a stone,
a cornerstone chosen and precious;
and whoever believes in him
will not be put to shame."

To you then who believe, he is precious; but for those who do not believe,

"The stone that the builders rejected
has become the very head of the corner,"

and

"A stone that makes them stumble,
and a rock that makes them fall."

They stumble because they disobey the word, as they were destined to do.

But you are a chosen race, a royal priesthood, a holy nation, God's own people, in order that you may proclaim the mighty acts of him who called you out of darkness into his marvelous light.

Once you were not a people,
but now you are God's people;
once you had not received mercy,
but now you have received mercy. (1 Pet. 2:4–10; cf. Isa. 28:16; Ps. 118:22; and Isa. 8:14–15)

This passage expounds upon the image of Christ the rock, rejected but now in place. In these later texts, God's enduring presence in Christ becomes the point. Jesus is always present, as a rock that never moves. Everything else can be built around this one stationary point of Jesus, who anchors the church around himself. Christ as cornerstone is a static image, and this is not what Paul is suggesting in 1 Corinthians 1—2. Christ crucified is not a cornerstone for faith. Although Paul uses the language of cornerstone and foundation, he contradicts that language, pointing to the limits of the foundational metaphor. Jesus does not stay put. This is one of the key messages of the crucifixion. God in Jesus does not remain; instead, God moves, and therefore God comes close and leaves. God was in human flesh in Jesus, and so God came close to us, but God also left, for to be human is to die. When Jesus' body was placed in a tomb, the tomb became empty, because God in Jesus did not stay in one place. Every place where Jesus once was is now empty; they have all been vacated. All that remains is the trace of where God and Jesus were. To build upon the empty places and to lay a foundation that is nothing but a trace is foolishness, to use Paul's term. Jesus does not stay put; instead, he moves as God incarnate. Jesus in constant motion becomes a stumbling block over which we trip because it is not where we last saw it or put it. It makes no sense, according to the wisdom of the age, because Jesus is not predictable, not static or stationary.

For the message about the cross is foolishness to those who are perishing, but to us who are being saved it is the power of God. For it is written,

"I will destroy the wisdom of the wise,
and the discernment of the discerning I will thwart."

Where is the one who is wise? Where is the scribe? Where is the debater of this age? Has not God made foolish the wisdom of the world? For since, in the wisdom of God, the world did not know God through wisdom, God decided, through the foolishness of our proclamation, to save those who believe. For Jews demand signs and Greeks desire wisdom, but we proclaim Christ crucified, a stumbling block to Jews and foolishness to Gentiles, but to those who are the called, both Jews and Greeks, Christ the power of God and the wisdom of God. For God's foolishness is wiser than human wisdom, and God's weakness is stronger than human strength. (1 Cor. 1:18–25; cf. Isa. 29:14)

As correct as it is to think of Jesus as foundation and cornerstone, Jesus is also stumbling block and foolishness. How is this a beginning of faith?

According to Paul, faith begins with fear.[3] Faith is born within just at the moment of abandonment, when we first combine the paradoxical sense that God was here and may still be here with the experience and feeling of God's absence. Before fear, there is no faith. There may be vision, there may be the experience of God's presence, but there is not faith. As the writer to the Hebrews expresses this, "faith is the assurance of things hoped for, the conviction of things not seen" (Heb. 11:1). When we see God, when we experience God's presence, when we know that God is with us in the flesh in Jesus, then we see. Hope has no purpose in the midst of presence. When God leaves, there is absence, abandonment, and fear of aloneness. We can no longer see God. In absence, hope and faith take the place that sight vacates. Thus, Paul preaches Christ crucified. Paul preaches that God incarnate died at human hands. Paul preaches God's absence,

---

[3]In the words of Israel's wisdom literature, "The fear of the LORD is the beginning of wisdom" (Prov. 9:10a; cf. 1:7). Perhaps this insight is not unlike Paul's concept of faith and foolishness, despite the difference in language and image.

for there is where faith occurs, in the fear driven by God's abandon-ment, when at the cross the body of God died and then disappeared.

The Body of Christ

In the early church's attempts to think about how believers re-lated to one another and to God in Jesus, some people developed the idea that we are like stones built into the temple in which God lives, as seen above in 1 Peter 2. When we are together, we are a strong structure, and God dwells in us, as a spirit who lives in a building. God lives in the temple, and Jesus is the cornerstone. However, this was not the only image that the early church used to describe their relationship with God and with each other. Elsewhere, Paul creates a provocative image: "My little children, for whom I am again in the pain of childbirth until Christ is formed in you..." (Gal. 4:19). Jesus grows within us, like a child growing in the womb.[4] This remarkably embodied image points to the continuing presence of God's Christ in us, in our bodies. Christ's body is here, inside us, growing. God is in the world once more. God did not leave us; God left us a seed that now grows until it is fully formed. In us as in Mary, the story of God's incarnation is ever beginning.

Paul does not develop this powerful sense of Christ growing in us. Instead, he uses the metaphor of a body to describe the church.

> For as in one body we have many members, and not all the members have the same function, so we, who are many, are one body in Christ, and individually we are members one of another. We have gifts that differ according to the grace given to us: prophecy, in proportion to faith; ministry, in minister-ing; the teacher, in teaching; the exhorter, in exhortation; the giver, in generosity; the leader, in diligence; the compas-sionate, in cheerfulness. (Rom. 12:4–8)

Here, the believers are one body, knit together because their dif-ferences are complementary. Together, we possess all the gifts that we need to survive as a community. As individuals, we have a need for each other and an investment in one another because our growth

---

[4]See Justo L. González, *When Christ Lives in Us: A Pilgrimage of Faith* (Nashville: Abingdon Press, 1995).

depends on each other, just as the growth and development of each part of the body depends on the nourishment it receives from the rest of the body.

The body lives and thrives because it is a community of differences. Paul comments that if every part of the body were a hand, the body would not do very well at all. Being a body requires differences. Each part has a different function. Each part has different needs. As contemporary science has learned more about the body, we have come to understand more about the body's needs. Some parts need certain vitamins, minerals, and chemicals to function well, but the same substance that keeps one part healthy may be toxic to another. The body is a delicate and ever-changing balance of competing forces.

Such is also true of the body of the believers. Individuals who are members of the one body will disagree with each other in terms of function and perspective. Some of these disagreements will be permanent and irresolvable. One part cannot transform into another, and one part cannot substitute for another. The parts of the body cannot learn to get along better or even at times learn to live next to each other. The ear cannot substitute for a tooth; ears and teeth will always have different functions, different perspectives, competing needs for nourishment, requirement for different chemicals, and an inability to understand what it is that the other does. The acids that allow the stomach to do its job would cause damage to other organs if they spilled over to them.

Likewise, in the church, some elements will think of other elements as destructive. Many parts will not understand what the others do and will disparage each other. Like white cells traveling the bloodstream devouring wayward particles, some parts of the church will damage other parts, and it will make sense only in the larger picture. None of us in the church has that larger picture. Some organs do seem encompassing, such as the skin, or connective, such as the nervous system. Some people within the church may understand more of the connections between the church's different groups than others, but this does not make their role any higher or better and certainly does not argue that the body would be better off if it were composed only of the skin and brain. The church's most rancorous and disagreeable members are every bit as necessary as the more beautiful, the more harmonious, the more integrative members. The true value of any part is never seen from within the body, and in most cases, it is not even visible outside the body.

In the human body, many parts probably do not realize that they are parts of the body. Some necessary parts—such as various parasites and bacteria that are vital to maintaining the body—are technically not parts of the human body, but are other creatures who inhabit the body. However, our survival depends on them. One wonders if there is a parallel within the church. Does every part of the body of Christ know that it is a part of the body? Or are there parts, even necessary parts, who would deny that they are a part of the body or even that the body exists? Are there equivalents to parasites and bacteria that are in codependent relationships with the body? The limits of the human body are difficult to discern, and such is likely to be true with the church as the body of Christ as well.

The book of Acts provides many portraits of what the church must be. The beginning of the church was characterized by magnificent growth, based in the church's sharing of all things in common.

> Awe came upon everyone, because many wonders and signs were being done by the apostles. All who believed were together and had all things in common; they would sell their possessions and goods and distribute the proceeds to all, as any had need. Day by day, as they spent much time together in the temple, they broke bread at home and ate their food with glad and generous hearts, praising God and having the goodwill of all the people. And day by day the Lord added to their number those who were being saved. (Acts 2:43–47)

Their unity led to their diversity, and their differences gave them reason to be together. There were great disagreements in those days, including councils that met together to try to settle differences (Acts 15). Coming together as one people occurred only because of the conflict, and through the conflict, they reached an agreement that they called unanimous (Acts 15:25). Everyone recognized the rightness of the decisions reached in unity that brought encouragement, strength, and peace, like a body unified (Acts 15:31–35). But immediately thereafter, there was sharp disagreement among the leaders, Paul and Barnabas, and they split because of their inability to share perspective (Acts 15:38–39). The conflicts of the church bring the church together; the unity of the church leads to conflict. This is the same way that bodies always work, operating in the struggle between unity and division. This occurs at the level of cells, which grow by division, and among the whole body, where intimate union leads to the division of birth. At all levels, unity and division are two parts of the reality of being a body.

The early church struggled with its differences, just as the present church does. There has never been perfect agreement, because the church is always a community that brings together differences. The earliest church included some who kept traditional dietary codes and others who thought that such regulations no longer pertained to Christians (Acts 10:9–32; cf. 1 Cor. 8). This was part of the wider conflict between Jews and Gentiles (Acts 10:34–48; Gal. 3:28; Eph. 2:11—3:6). Cultural divisions of every sort threatened to fragment the church, but the church thrived on these differences.

The church is a body of great dissension and huge conflict, held together in precarious balance. Yet it is one body, even though so many of its parts would never understand that, nor should they be asked to do so, for that would betray their own function. This body of believers, Paul writes, is "in Christ." We are one body in Christ (Rom. 12:5; cf. Eph. 4:15–16). However, when Paul develops this idea about the church to a much greater extent in 1 Corinthians 12, he makes an additional point.

> For just as the body is one and has many members, and all the members of the body, though many, are one body, so it is with Christ. For in the one Spirit we were all baptized into one body—Jews or Greeks, slaves or free—and we were all made to drink of one Spirit.
>
> . . . .
>
> Now you are the body of Christ and individually members of it. (1 Cor. 12:12–13, 27)

Paul still emphasizes that believers are connected together in the same way that a body is connected. But now he also says that we are the body of Christ.[5] This body of which Paul has been speaking, which is the church, is the body of Christ. Even though Jesus' body

---

[5]See Ronald E. Osborn, *In Christ's Place: Christian Ministry in Today's World* (St. Louis: Bethany Press, 1967), especially 179–93.

disappeared after death and resurrection, Paul continues to write of the body of Christ as a present reality, but now with the sense that the body of Christ is the church.[6]

This same understanding of the church as the body of Christ permeates Paul's discussion of communion in Christian practice:

> The cup of blessing that we bless, is it not a sharing in the blood of Christ? The bread that we break, is it not a sharing in the body of Christ? Because there is one bread, we who are many are one body, for we all partake of the one bread.
>
> ....
>
> For I received from the Lord what I also handed on to you, that the Lord Jesus on the night when he was betrayed took a loaf of bread, and when he had given thanks, he broke it and said, "This is my body that is for you. Do this in remembrance of me." In the same way he took the cup also, after supper, saying, "This cup is the new covenant in my blood. Do this, as often as you drink it, in remembrance of me." For as often as you eat this bread and drink the cup, you proclaim the Lord's death until he comes. (1 Cor. 10:16–17; 11:23–26)

When the church partakes of communion, the cup of wine is the sharing in the blood of Christ and the bread is a sharing in the body of Christ. This is true for Paul in two ways, it seems. First, the people who gather together for that meal of remembrance are partaking together of wine and bread that symbolize and represent the blood and body of Christ; the people share together in the meal that they eat. Second, the people share together being the blood and body of Christ. The meal of communion is much more than eating at the same time. Paul makes that clear in his condemnation of those who share the meal together but who have contempt for each other (1 Cor. 11:17–22). Communion brings people together in more ways because they share a role as members of the body of Christ. One might even say that the Lord's supper is an act of membering and re-membering, in

---

[6]Cf. Mark C. Taylor, Erring: *A Postmodern A/Theology* (Chicago: University of Chicago Press, 1984), 141: "Posthumous people are called to live the death of the self."

the sense of bringing together the members of the body of Christ. As one, the individuals who eat this meal together become Christ's body.

Paul reflects that those who share the meal of communion "proclaim the Lord's death until he comes" (1 Cor. 11:26). Paul does not focus attention on the risen Christ, but instead on the crucified Lord Jesus. Jesus' death leaves behind a body—the body of Christ that is the church. The group of believers is the remnant of God's incarnation, the trace of God's presence, the very remains of God in the world. God has raised Jesus from the dead and breathed spirit once more into the body of Christ, and we are that body.

God's Present Incarnation

God is incarnate in the world today in the body of Christ. The church becomes the physical presence of God in the world. What God does in the world, whatever actions of God take physical human form, are actions performed by God's body.

This line of thinking is dangerous, especially because it can slide into arrogance. Paul equates the church with the body of Christ, which is the body of Jesus crucified, which is the body of God incarnate. The idea of the church as God incarnate, however, can tempt us to think of the church as the only manifestation of God's presence. Combined with arrogance, this belief could encourage a rejection of the other ways in which God is present. We could emphasize God's incarnation in the church and use that emphasis to exclude and demean religious groups that do not agree with our particular views and who do things that we might not understand as being part of the body of Christ. Similarly, understanding the church as God's body could feed some of the church's long-standing hatreds, especially of Jews and of the created world. God's full incarnation in the church does not mean that the church is the only way God is present. God is much more than can ever be expressed in human form or human institutions, even in the church that is the body of Christ. Just as the gospel of John quoted Jesus' saying that he was a shepherd who had other flocks of sheep (John 10:16), God's incarnation in the church means that God may well be incarnate in other places as well. God's perpetual habit of surprising humanity with presence means that God is likely to be found in more places than we have ever realized. But at the same time, we as the church are God's body, with the full experience and responsibility of being not only God's people but the very physical presence of God in the world today. Whatever God should do in the world, we as God's body should do. In incarnation as the body of Christ, we share with God completely the tasks and purposes that God has undertaken throughout the ages.

In ancient times, the Israelites wrote stories of God as present in the flesh. God walked in Eden's garden; God parented the children of Israel, as well as the child Ishmael. Those old stories portrayed God as present in the flesh. These images of God as incarnate carry through the tradition of scripture to its very end when God sets a table for all at the end of the book of Revelation. God also works through people—although not always through the leaders whom we expect and elect. In fact, God's work with people often occurs best at the margins, not in the centers of human power, which are more sensitive to their agendas and the maintenance of their own human privilege than they are responsive to God's desires for the world. God is also present in the spirit, in ways that shock, surprise, and motivate, for the spirit blows through our lives like a wind that is unpredictable, sometimes destructive, always refreshing and empowering. The whole experience of God as present in our lives can be traumatic, for God refuses our prediction, resists our desires that God play by our rules, and confounds the understanding of our best-trained minds and our most faithful hearts. God is truly an other, not like us—yet God desires us.

In the New Testament, God's incarnation takes the form of Jesus. In this way, we see God among us and we hear clearly God's repetition of the ancient prophetic statements of God's desires for the world. God desires that we join in the transformation of the world, and God explains what this transformation can offer and what it will cost. God even demonstrates that cost, for human rejection of God's desires seems inevitable and culminates in the crucifixion of Jesus. Yet crucifixion is not the end. The death of Jesus and the disappearance of God's incarnate body in the world leaves three sets of traces: the sightings of Jesus' resurrected body for a few weeks or months, the presence of the spirit that had always been among God's people but is freshly experienced in Jesus' absence, and the church as the body of Christ and as God's continually incarnate presence in the world.

God's incarnation takes many forms within the biblical witness. God has always been and will continue to be present in human flesh in God's own body, in the body of Jesus, and in the church that is the body of Christ. God is present in the world through spirit and through people who follow that spirit. God is incarnate in the world through believers today.

The body of God goes beyond those who believe. A cell does not need to understand that it is part of the body or to believe in the body or to love the body. It is enough that the cell function as a cell, and thus is part of the body. Likewise, God's body extends far past the believers who identify themselves as God's body. All people become essential elements of God's body, removing the barriers we construct of gender, race, class, age, language, creed, and ability. God's body is all of us.

Furthermore, God's body is more than just the human. All creatures are expressions of God, and God's body ties us together with animals and other living creatures. The ecology of the world is fully within God.[7] All things animate and inanimate in the world and throughout the cosmos together make up God's body. In fact, God's body is large enough and pervasive enough to include all the world, even all the universe.

In this sense, God is revealed in all of us. In fact, all creation is necessary to begin to manifest the full being of God. People of all varieties, whether we like them or not, are vital parts of God's body. God is incarnate in all, whether they realize it or not. God lives within the universe, from the vast galaxies to the smallest subatomic particles.

The cosmic body of God is a rich metaphor, showing the vastness of God beyond our experience. But the image of God as a body is ultimately personal. God is in a form we can know and love, even if we cannot quite understand.

One of the letters written to the early church contained this cryptic sentence: "when God is revealed, we will be like God, for we will see God as God is" (1 John 3:2). Seeing God for God's self is almost the same as being like God. For those who live as part of God's body, it makes sense that seeing God and seeing the self are just about the same thing. God's incarnation among us and in us brings God amazingly near, almost too near to see or touch. When we do see God, we know that God has been among us all along. Incarnation began at the same moment as creation and continues to the end of the age. God's

---

[7]See Sallie McFague, *Models of God: Theology for an Ecological, Nuclear Age* (Philadelphia: Fortress Press, 1987), 11 and throughout. McFague understands "the world as God's body to which God is present as mother, lover, and friend of the last and the least in all of creation" (87). See also, Idem, *The Body of God: An Ecological Theology* (Minneapolis: Fortress Press, 1993), especially 133.

body remains in the world today, and its tasks are our tasks. We have longed to know God, to see God, to touch God, and to love God, and in the end we find that God has been present, within us and us within God's body, all along.

Our desire for God has changed us. We have longed for God until we have seen God and have become made new in God's image, with God's body. Now that we are the body of Christ, God's own body, God lives on in us and will not go away. We live as God's body. In our striving for God's tasks, we are unstoppable; in our partnership with God, we are eternal, because we have become the body of Christ. The first letter of John states this similarly:

> We declare to you what was from the beginning, what we have heard, what we have seen with our eyes, what we have looked at and touched with our hands, concerning the word of life—this life was revealed, and we have seen it and testify to it, and declare to you the eternal life that was with God and was revealed to us—we declare to you what we have seen and heard so that you also may have fellowship with us; and truly our fellowship is with God and God's Son Jesus Christ. We are writing these things so that our joy may be complete. (1 John 1:1–4)

When we see and touch God, as we have sought to do from the very beginning, we touch life and we bring that life within us through the connections we have with each other. And our joy is complete. We have seen and touched God; we have shared heart and purpose. Now, since we are the body of Christ, we have come so close to God that we will never be apart. The boundaries have been broken down; the spaces between us and God have been removed. This has happened in Christ's flesh, in the body of God, where we are now united, reconciled, and combined.

> For Christ is our peace; in his flesh he has made both groups into one and has broken down the dividing wall, that is, the hostility between us. He has abolished the law with its commandments and ordinances, that he might create in himself one new humanity in place of the two, thus making peace, and might reconcile both groups to God in one body through the cross, thus putting to death that hostility through it. (Eph. 2:14–16)

Humanity ends its divisions as it ends its separation from God in one body, the body of Christ that died on the cross and lives in the church. We are as close as a part of God's own body. God is incarnate in us, God's people, who have carried the image of God from creation's first moment and who have now become more like God as God is revealed in us. Our longing turns to delight in this union within God's body.

From the stories of the most ancient days in Eden's garden, to the story of the life and death of Jesus the Messiah, and onward in the continuing story of the church's life in partnership with God, we have been in God's image and God has been in human flesh. As God has been incarnate and has learned through life and death what it means to be human, we have learned what it means to become one with the body of God. Incarnation is more than just God's presence with us, past or present. It is a shared life, a common task, a unity with purpose, a single goal in our multiple visions. Yet it is even more. As God taught us to walk as humans, as we witnessed God's first steps as incarnate human, now we walk hand in hand with God. With the hesitant steps of children, God's children, we learn to walk in God's own body.

Scripture Index